THE ECHOES OF RAGNAROK

A coloring adventure through the End Times
of Norse Mythology

First Printing, 2023
Clayton A. Pelton (Hellpigeon Studios)
1554 Keily Run
Tallahasse, FL 32301

Social Media Links and Support Pages:
https://www.facebook.com/claytonapelton
https://ko-fi.com/hellpigeonstudios
https://www.patreon.com/HellpigeonStudios
https://www.buymeacoffee.com/hellpigeonstudios

"The Norns"

Three powerful, mystical beings who shape the destiny of gods and men.
They dwell at the base of the world tree, Yggdrasil, in the well of Urd.
The eldest, Urd, represents the past; Verdandi, the middle sister,
embodies the present; and Skuld, the youngest, signifies the future.
They weave the tapestry of fate, carving runes into Yggdrasil's bark,
infusing it with their decrees. Their appearance is majestic yet enigmatic,
often depicted as wise, ageless women, each holding attributes that
symbolize their dominion over time. They are revered and feared, for
their decisions are irreversible and profound.

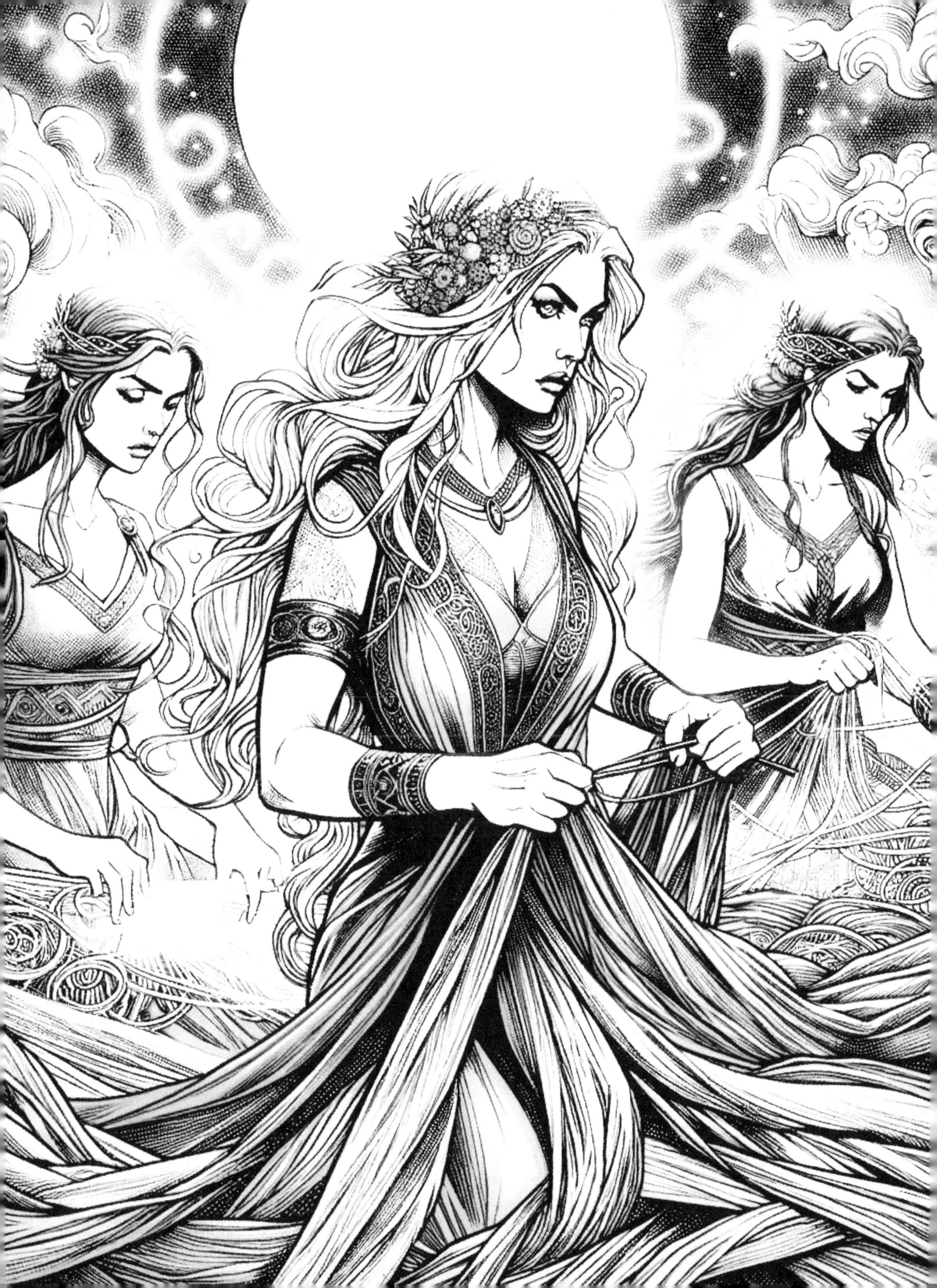

"Fimbulwinter"

A terrifying, relentless winter that precedes the end of the world, known as Ragnarok. It consists of three successive winters, lacking any summer in between, plunging the world into darkness and cold. This brutal winter symbolizes the world's descent into chaos and conflict. During Fimbulwinter, snowstorms ravage the earth, temperatures plummet to life-threatening levels, and the sun becomes a distant memory. It's a time of despair, as famine and strife grip the world, setting the stage for the final battle. Fimbulwinter's harshness signifies the old world's death, making way for rebirth after Ragnarok.

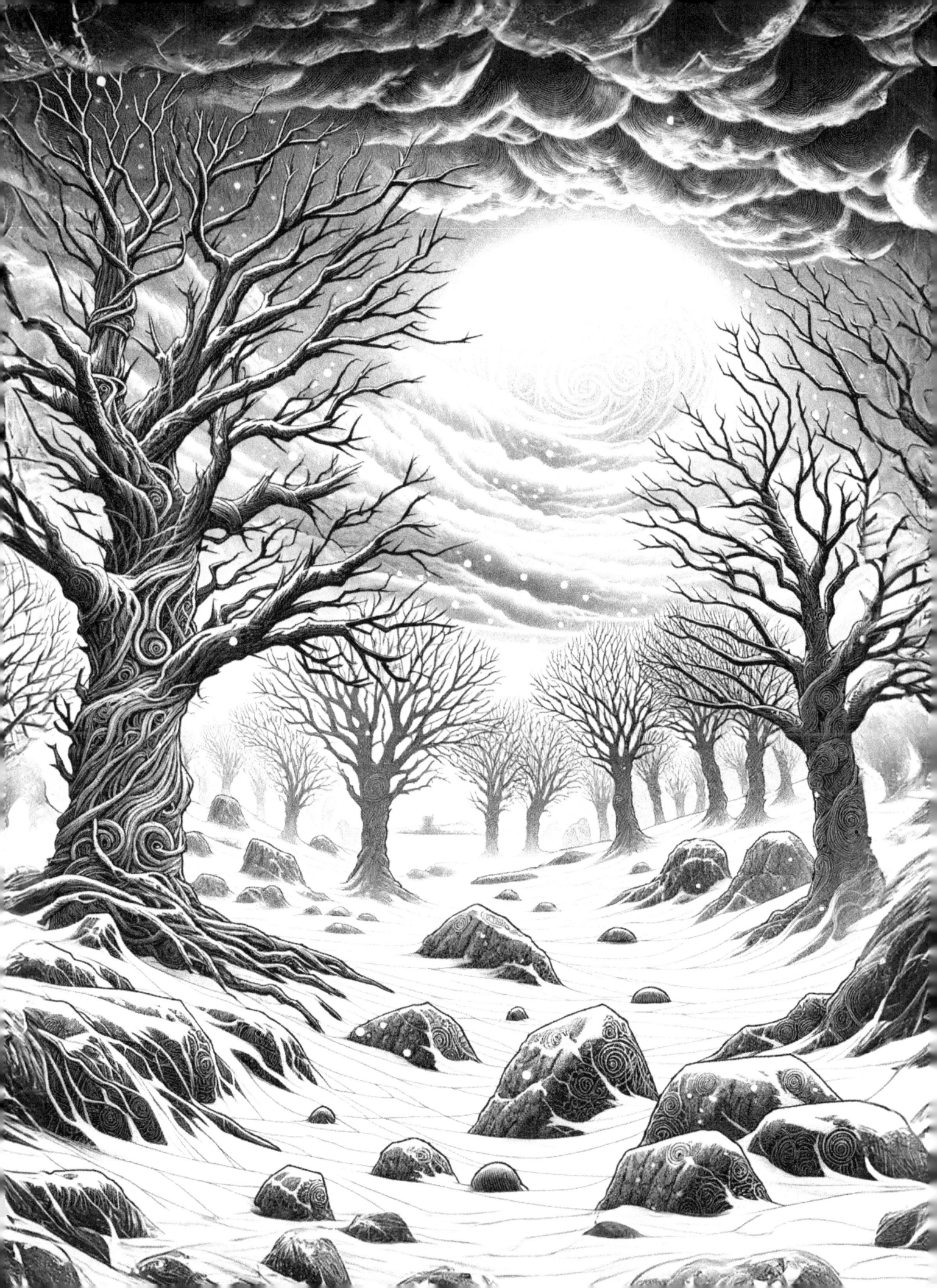

"The Devouring of the Sun and the Moon"

The celestial bodies are pursued relentlessly by two monstrous wolves, Skoll and Hati. Skoll chases the Sun, and Hati hunts the Moon, both driven by a cosmic hunger. As Ragnarok unfolds, the wolves finally catch their celestial quarries. Skoll engulfs the Sun, plunging the world into an eerie darkness, while Hati devours the Moon, snuffing out its silvery glow. This catastrophic act signals the beginning of the end, a pivotal moment when the cosmos descends into chaos, ushering in a period of unparalleled upheaval and transformation.

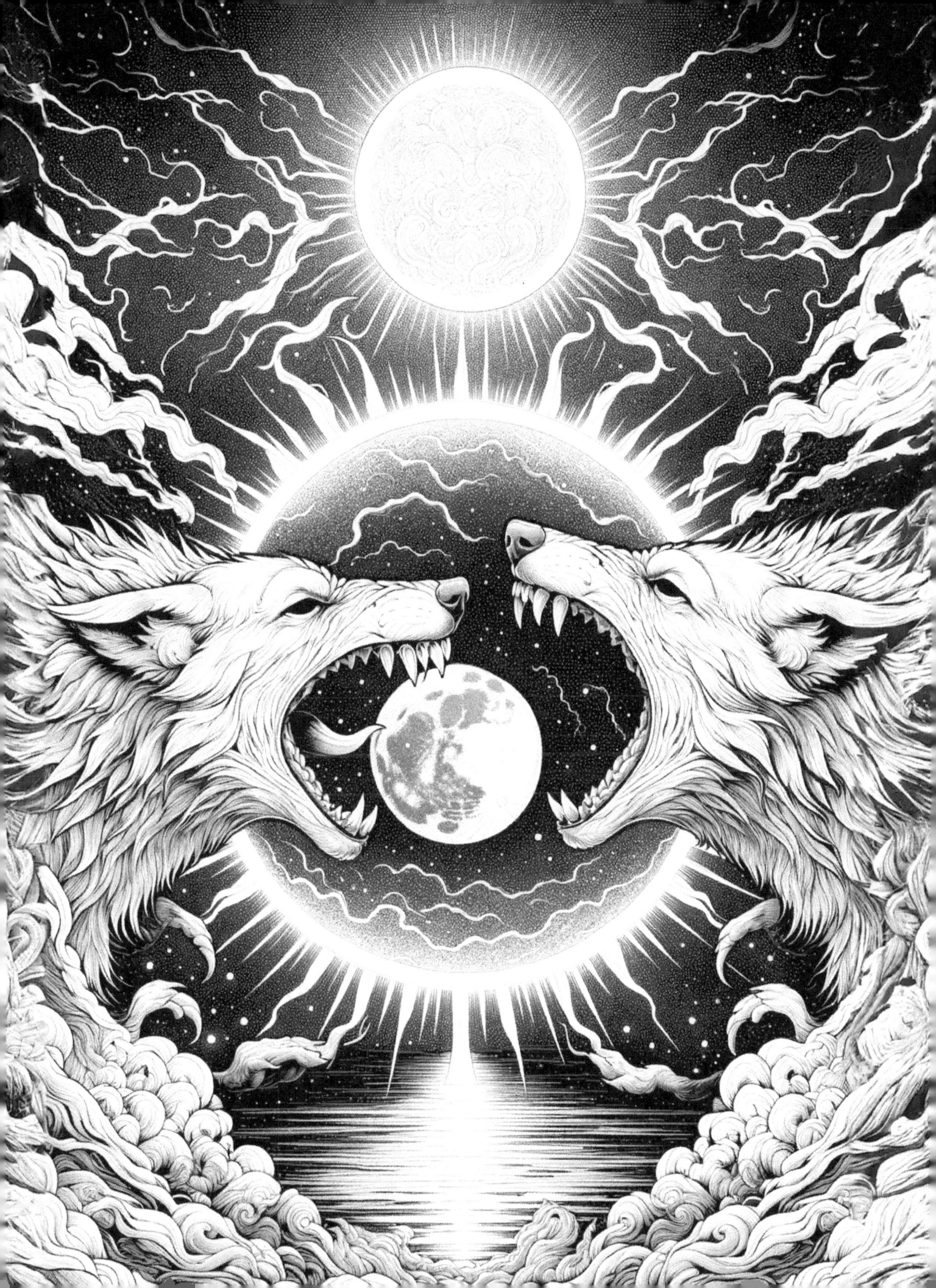

"Baldr the Bright"

The shining god of light, joy, purity, and beauty. The son of Odin and Frigg, he is distinguished by his radiant complexion and his kind, merciful nature. Baldr's hall, Breidablik, is the brightest in Asgard, reflecting his luminous spirit. His tragic death, caused by a mistletoe arrow manipulated by the trickster god Loki, marks one of the most poignant tales. Baldr's demise, mourned by all of creation, is a harbinger of Ragnarok, the end of times. Despite this, his return after Ragnarok symbolizes hope, renewal, and the triumph of light over darkness.

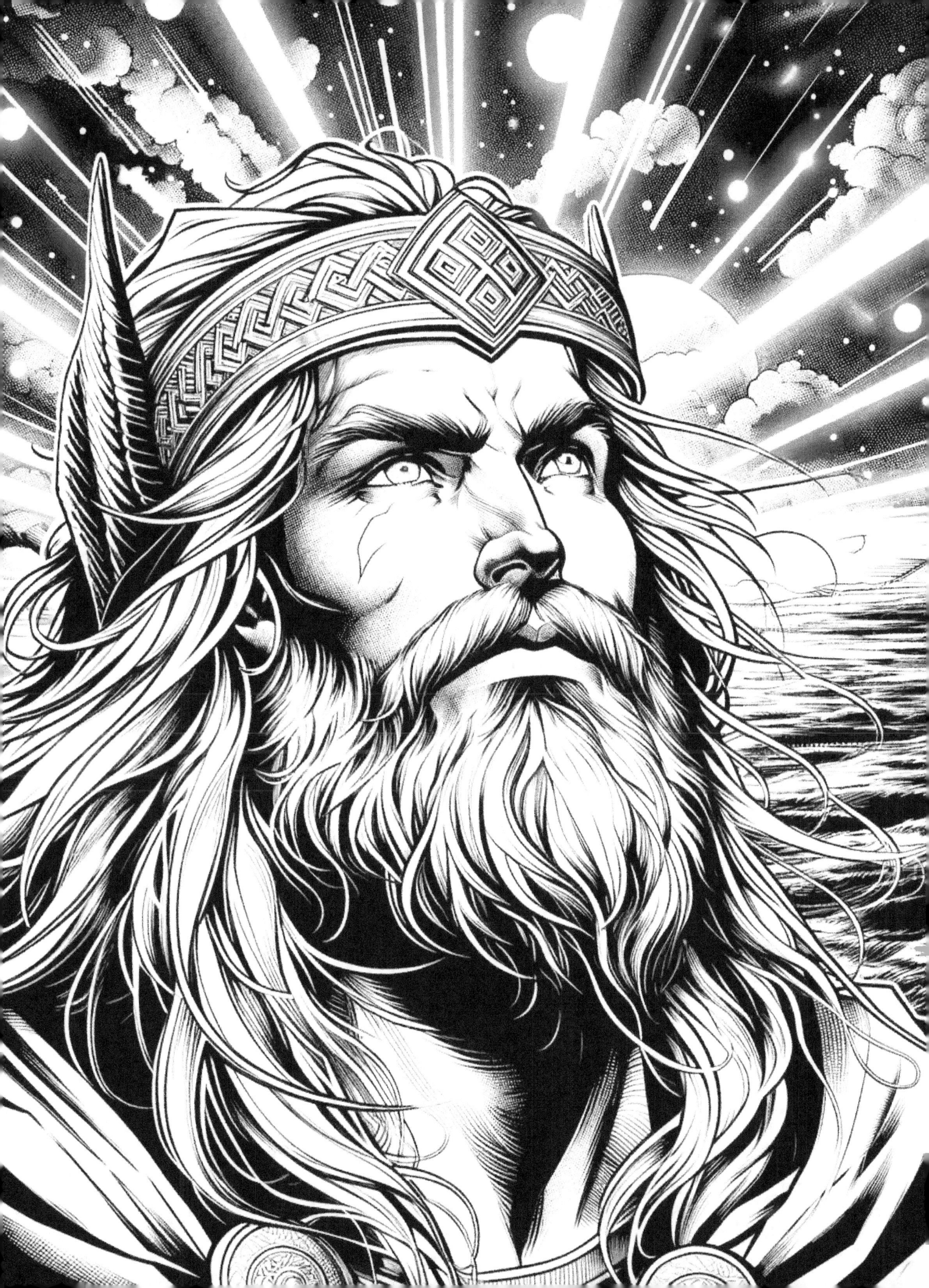

"Baldr's Hall, Breidablik"

The magnificent hall of Baldr, the god of light and purity. Nestled in Asgard, the realm of the gods, Breidablik stands out for its unrivaled beauty and splendor. It is said to have the finest architecture, with walls and rooftops made of precious metals, shining brightly under the sun. The hall embodies Baldr's own attributes of brightness and purity, as only the purest of hearts can reside within it. Surrounded by peaceful, idyllic landscapes, Breidablik is a symbol of tranquility, a sanctuary untouched by deception or evil, reflecting the noble spirit of its divine inhabitant.

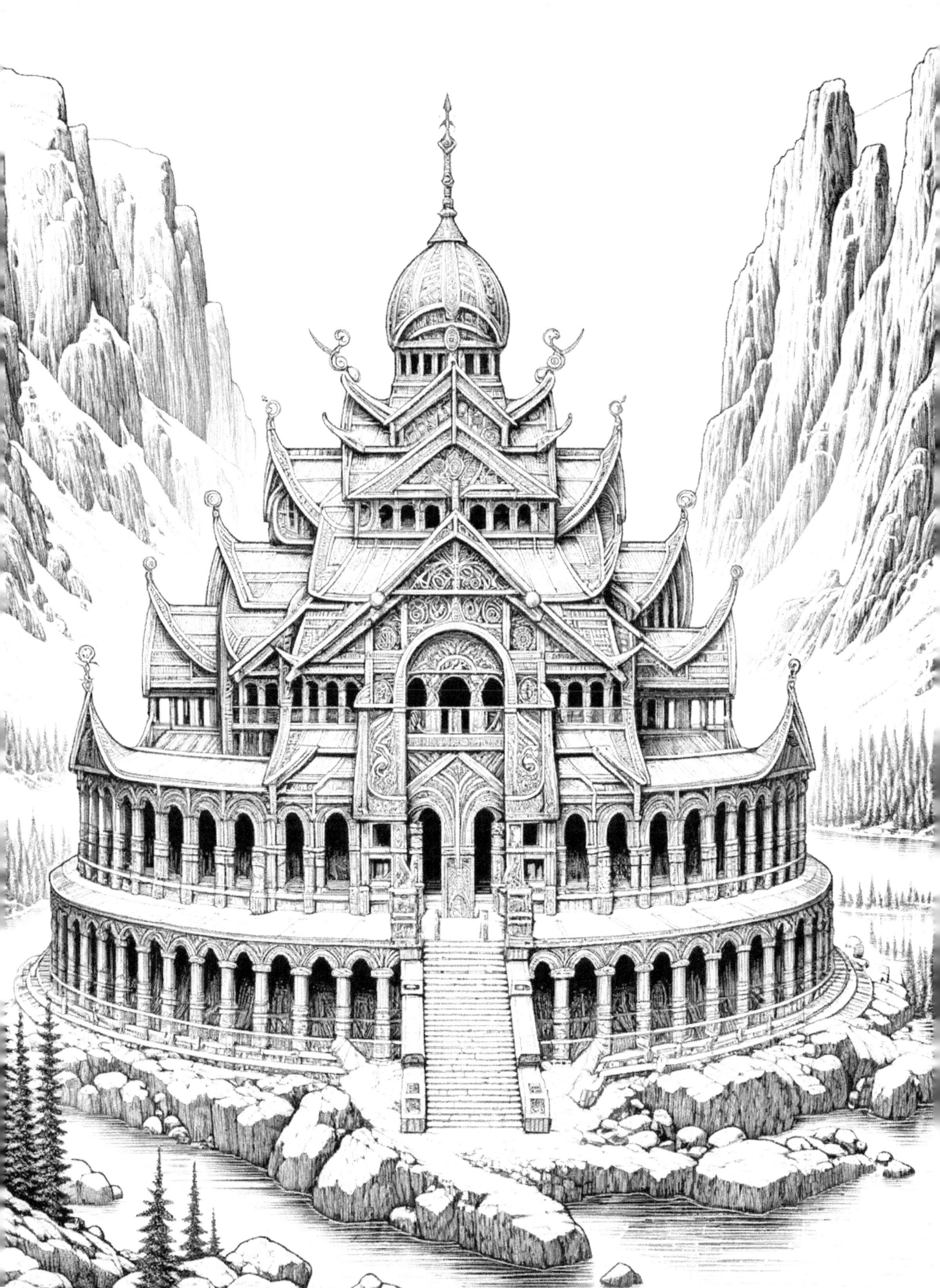

"The Tragic Deception"

The tragedy of Baldr's death unfolds with his blind brother, Hodr. Mischievously orchestrated by Loki, the gods, confident in Baldr's invincibility, throw objects at him in jest. Loki, envious and cunning, discovers Baldr's only vulnerability: mistletoe. He crafts a dart from this plant and guides Hodr's hand to shoot Baldr. The mistletoe pierces Baldr, bringing about his untimely demise. This act, born from Loki's deceit and Hodr's unwitting participation, strikes sorrow and despair into the heart of Asgard, marking a pivotal moment in the cosmic saga, leading towards the cataclysmic event of Ragnarok.

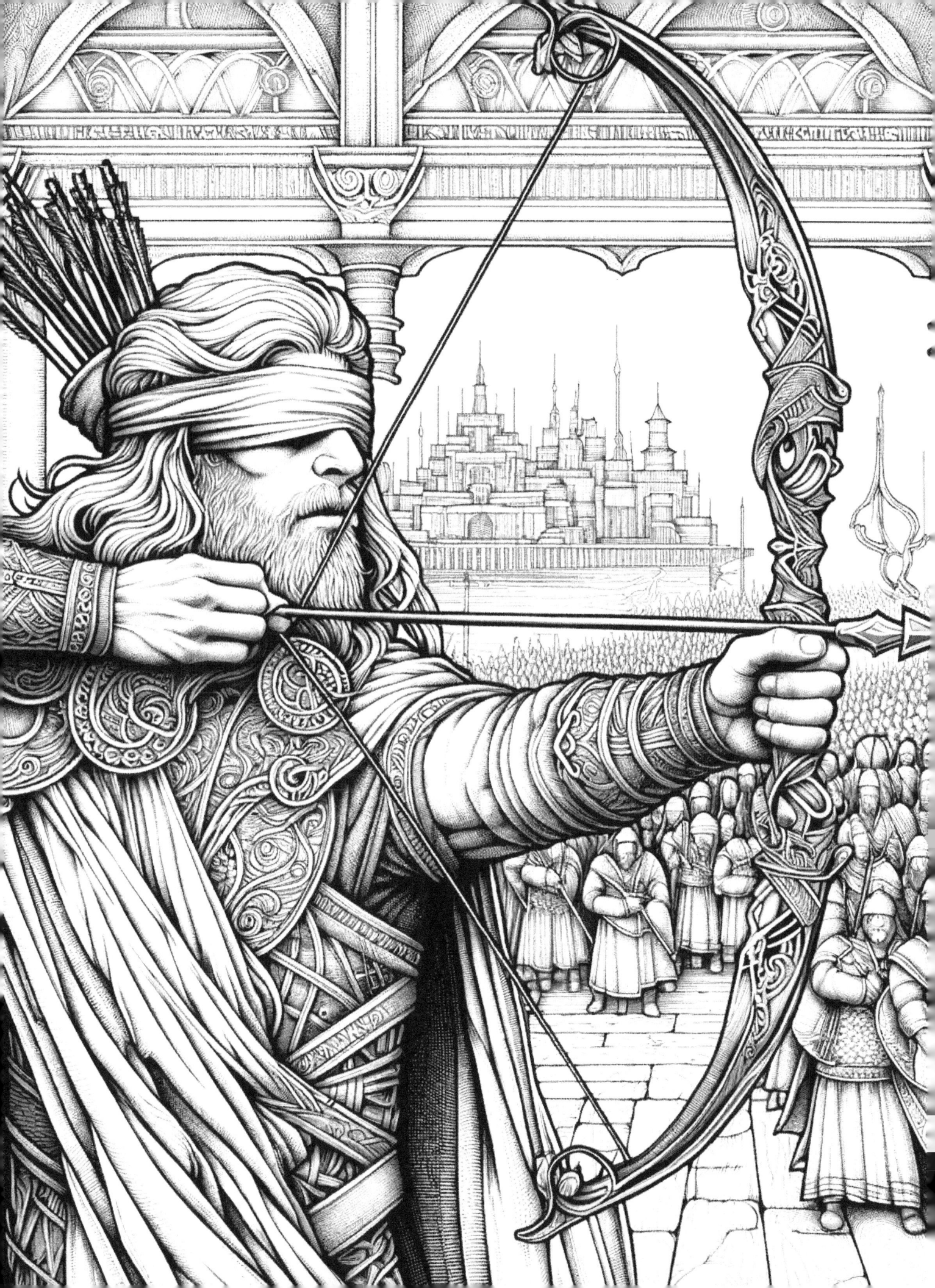

"Asgard"

The celestial fortress of the Aesir gods, a realm of grandeur and might. Perched in the heavens, it is accessible only via Bifrost, the rainbow bridge. Asgard's majestic halls, like Odin's Valhalla and Thor's Thrudheim, echo with the tales of gods and heroes. Surrounded by impregnable walls built by a giant, it stands as a symbol of strength and protection. Within its boundaries, gods convene to discuss fates and battles, amidst verdant gardens and splendid palaces. Asgard, a nexus of divine power and wisdom, is the epitome of the gods' glory and their eternal struggle against chaos.

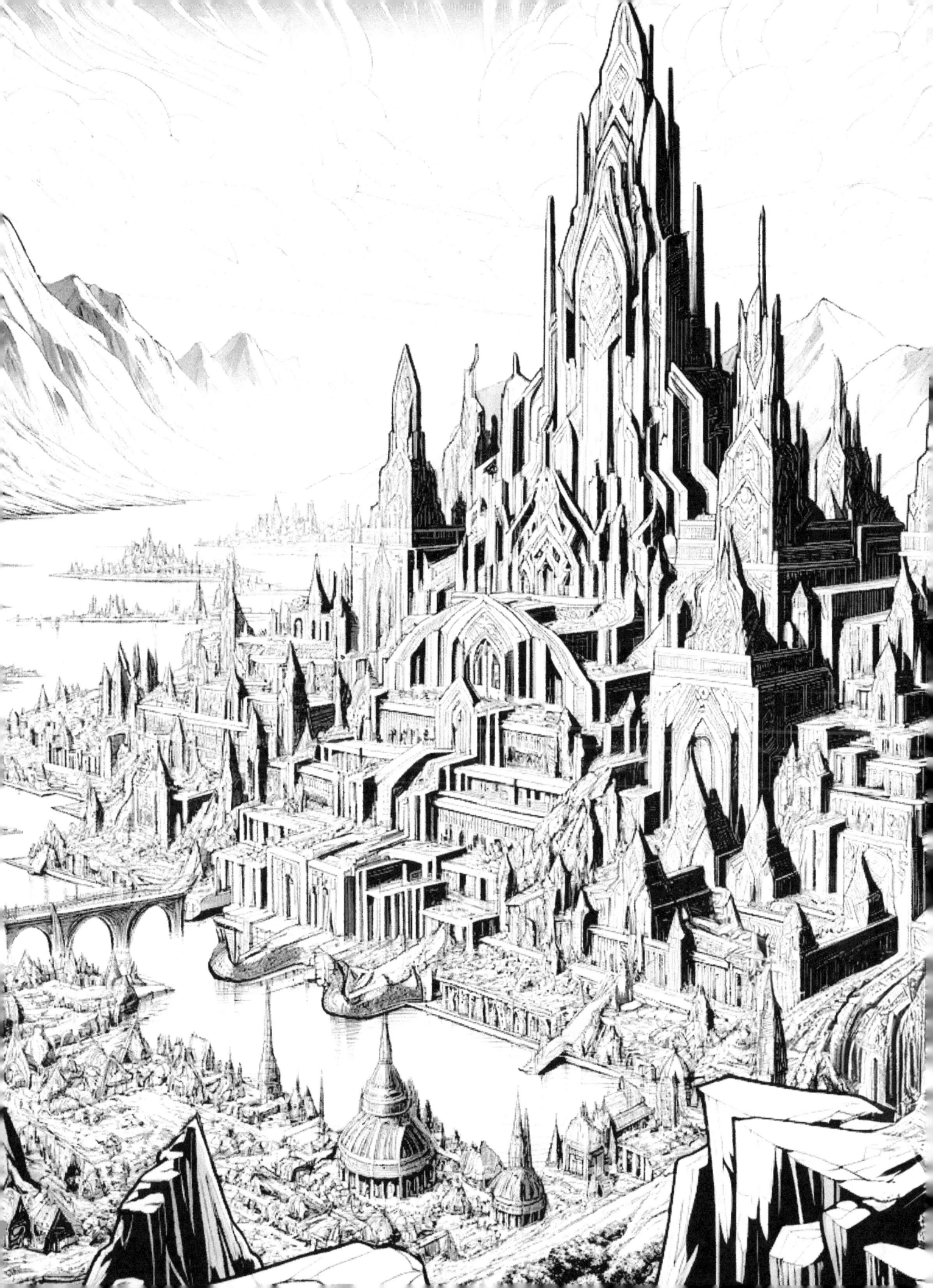

"Odin"

The Allfather and chief of the Aesir gods, is famously associated with two ravens named Huginn and Muninn. These names translate to "Thought" (Huginn) and "Memory" (Muninn). Every day, Odin sends them out at dawn to fly all over the world, known as Midgard. Upon their return, they perch on Odin's shoulders and whisper into his ears all the news and happenings they have seen and heard. This allows Odin to be omniscient, keeping him informed about the affairs of not just the gods and the heavens but also of humans. The ravens symbolize Odin's intellectual and spiritual powers, emphasizing his role as a god of wisdom, knowledge, and war.

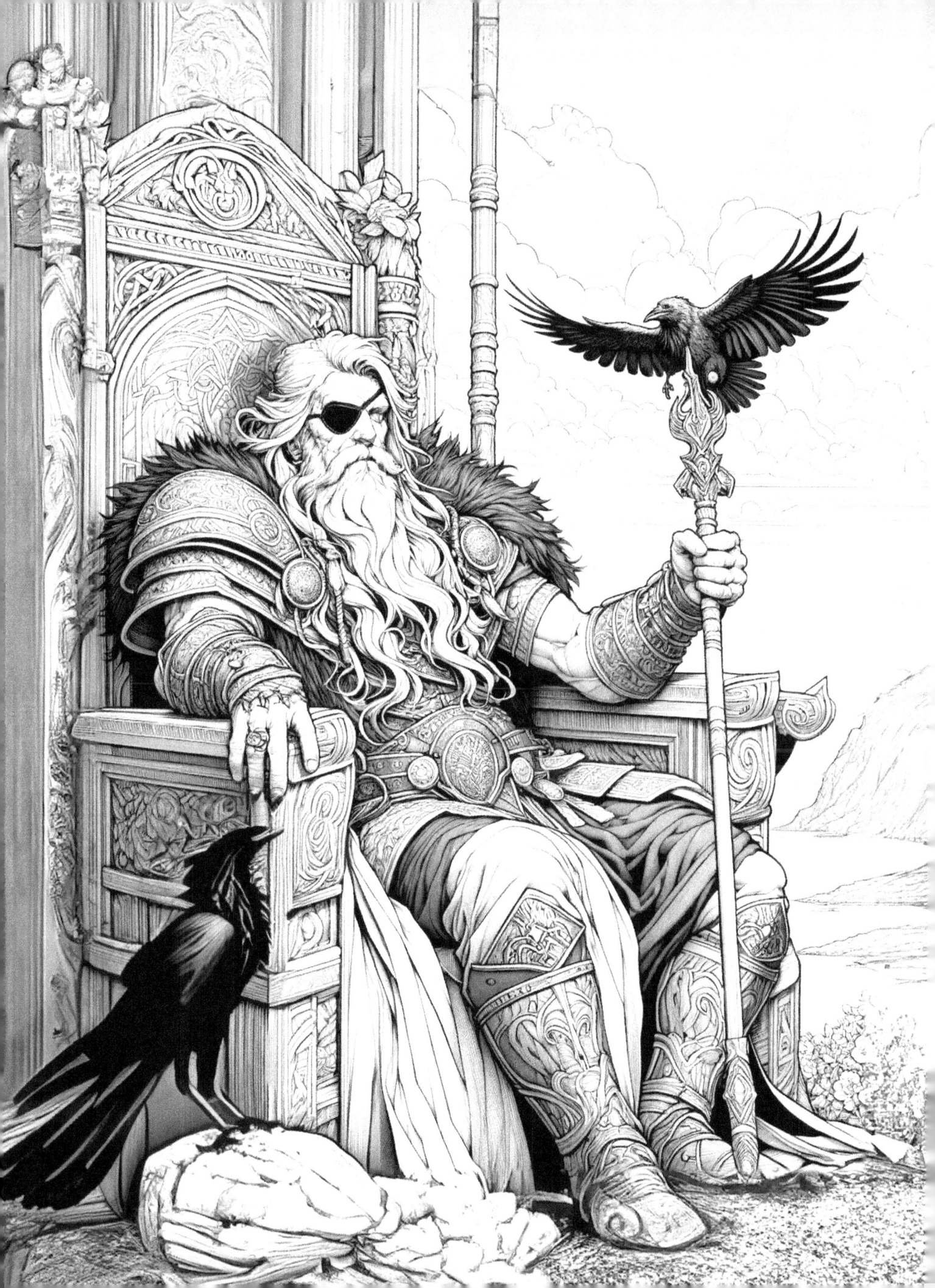

"Frigg"

The revered queen of the Aesir exuded wisdom and grace. As Odin's wife, she held a paramount position among the gods. Her foresight and knowledge of destiny were unmatched, yet she was discreet about her insights. Frigg's domain encompassed marriage, motherhood, and domestic life, and she was a loving and protective mother to Baldr, the god of light. Her enduring love for her son played a central role in the tragic tale of Baldr's death. Frigg's influence, as a divine matriarch, embodied the nurturing, and importance of family and fate in their world.

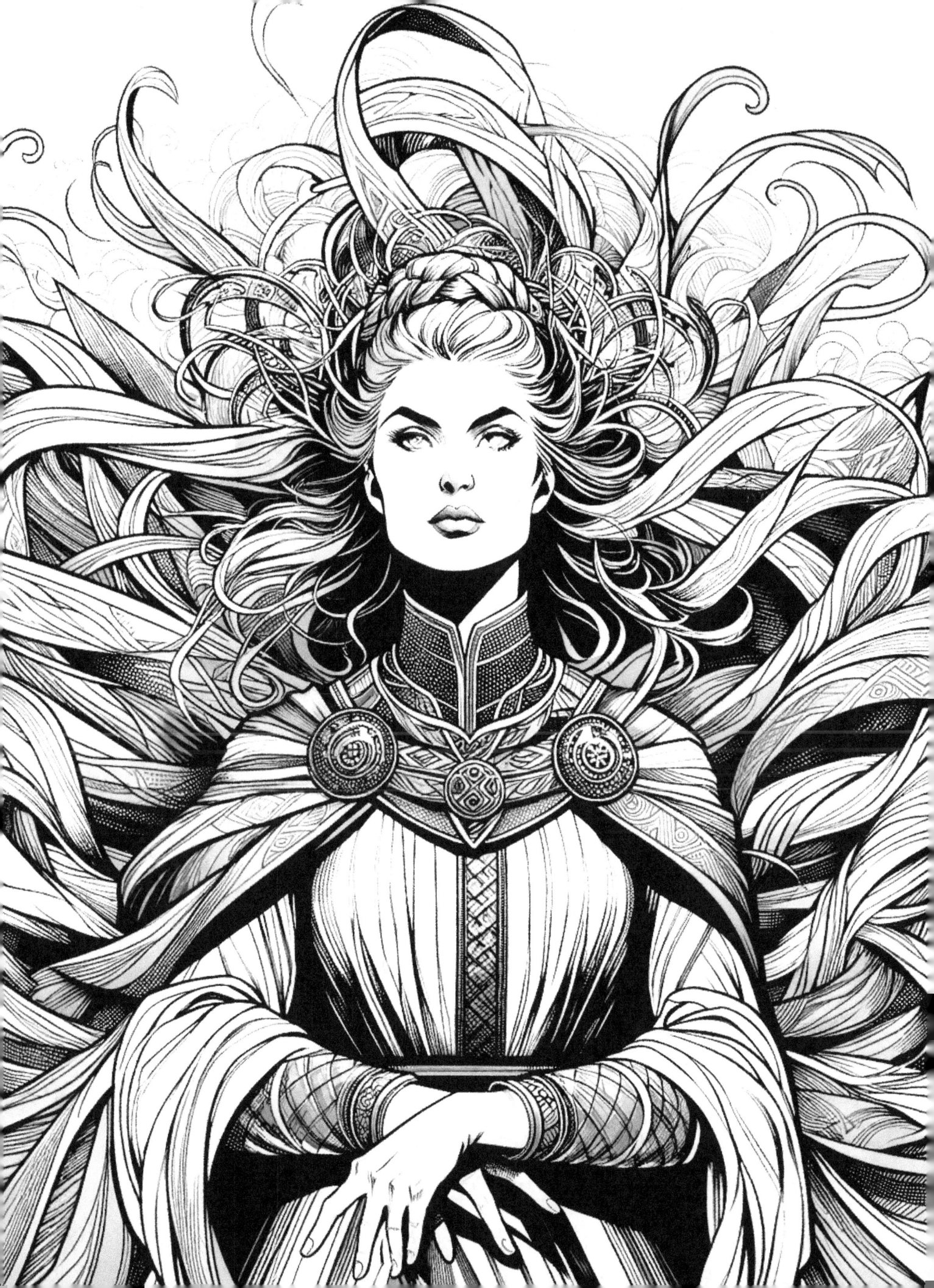

"Valhalla"

Valhalla is the glorious hall of Odin, where he welcomes the warriors who die bravely in battle. Valhalla is located in Asgard, and it is a huge palace with a roof made of shields and a hall that can fit thousands of guests. The warriors, called Einherjar, enjoy endless feasts of boar meat and mead, served by the valkyries, the beautiful maidens who choose the slain. They also fight each other every day for fun and practice, until the day of Ragnarok, when they will join Odin in the final war against the forces of chaos.

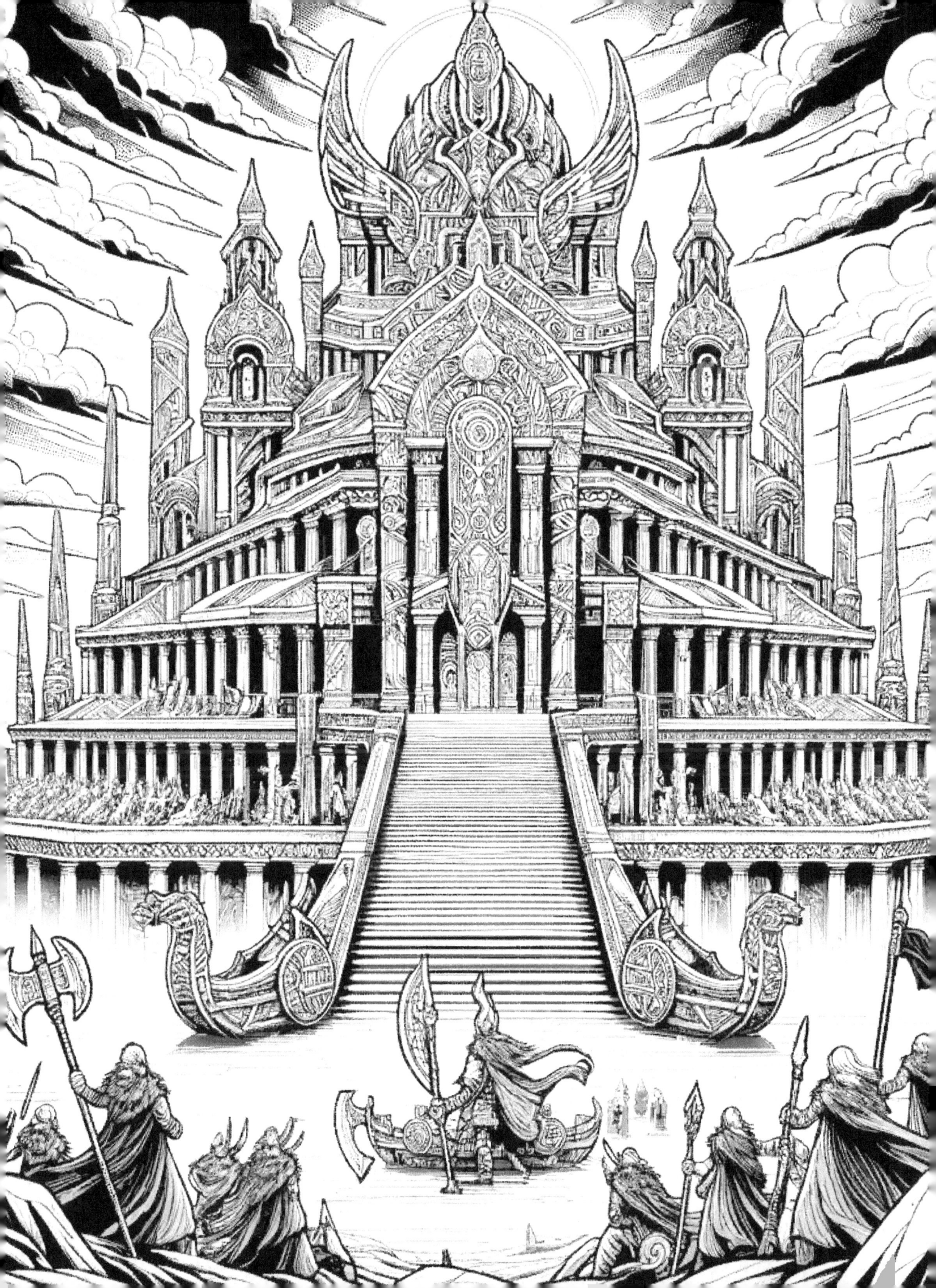

"The Valkyrie"

The warrior maidens of Odin, the king of the gods. They fly over the battlefields, mounted on horses, wolves, or boars, and armed with spears and shields. They have the power to choose who lives and who dies in combat, and they escort the souls of the fallen heroes to Valhalla, the hall of the slain. There, the valkyries serve mead to the warriors, who prepare for the final battle of Ragnarok, when they will fight alongside Odin against the forces of evil. The valkyries are also known as wish-maidens, as they fulfill Odin's wishes.

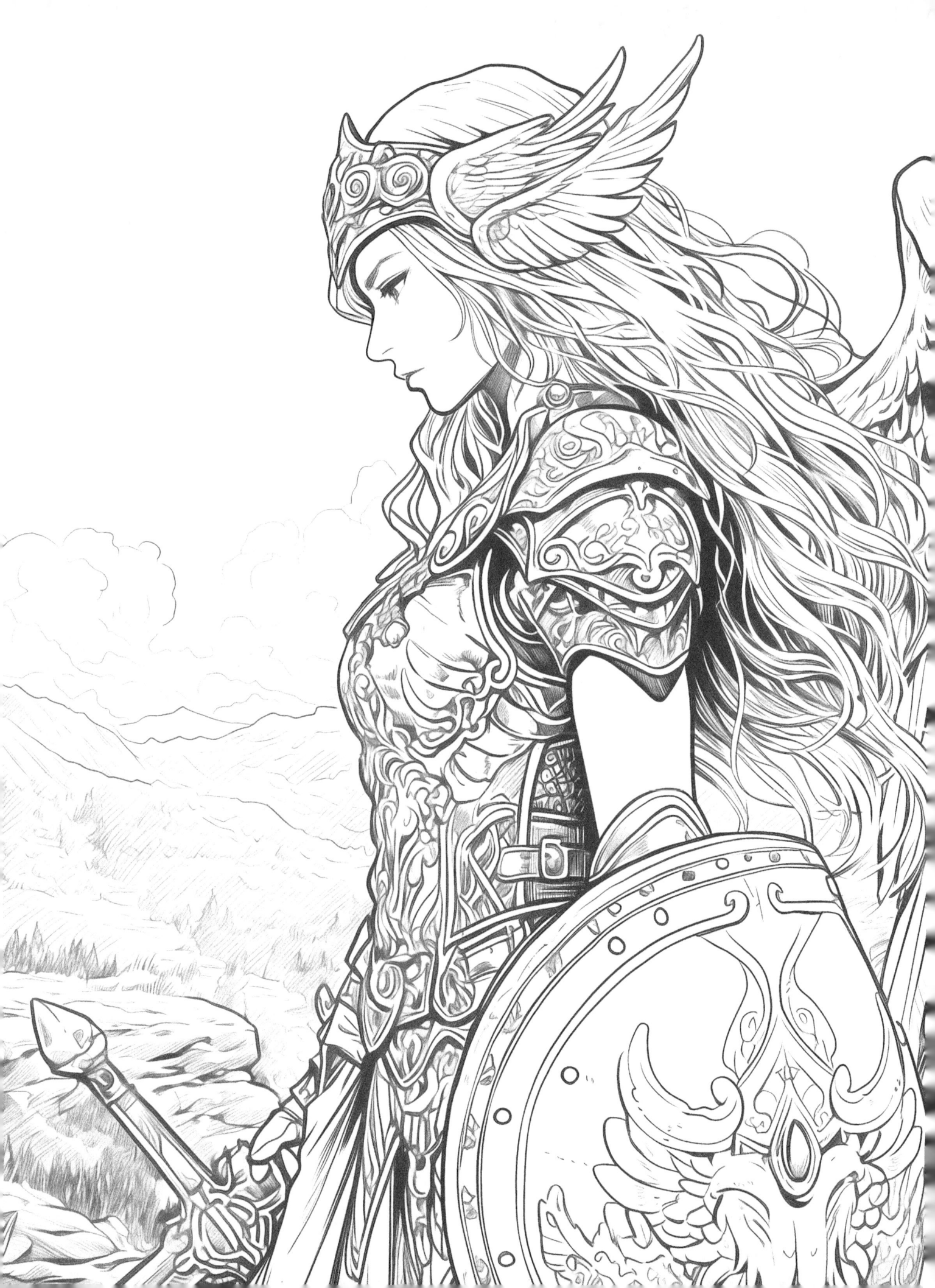

"The Einherjar"

The chosen ones, the brave and loyal fighters who died in glory on the battlefield. They are welcomed by Odin, the king of the gods, to his hall of Valhalla, where they feast and drink with the valkyries, the beautiful wish-maidens. They are not at rest, though, for they train and fight every day, preparing for the final battle of Ragnarok, when they will stand by Odin's side against the forces of chaos. They are the elite army of the gods, the lone warriors.

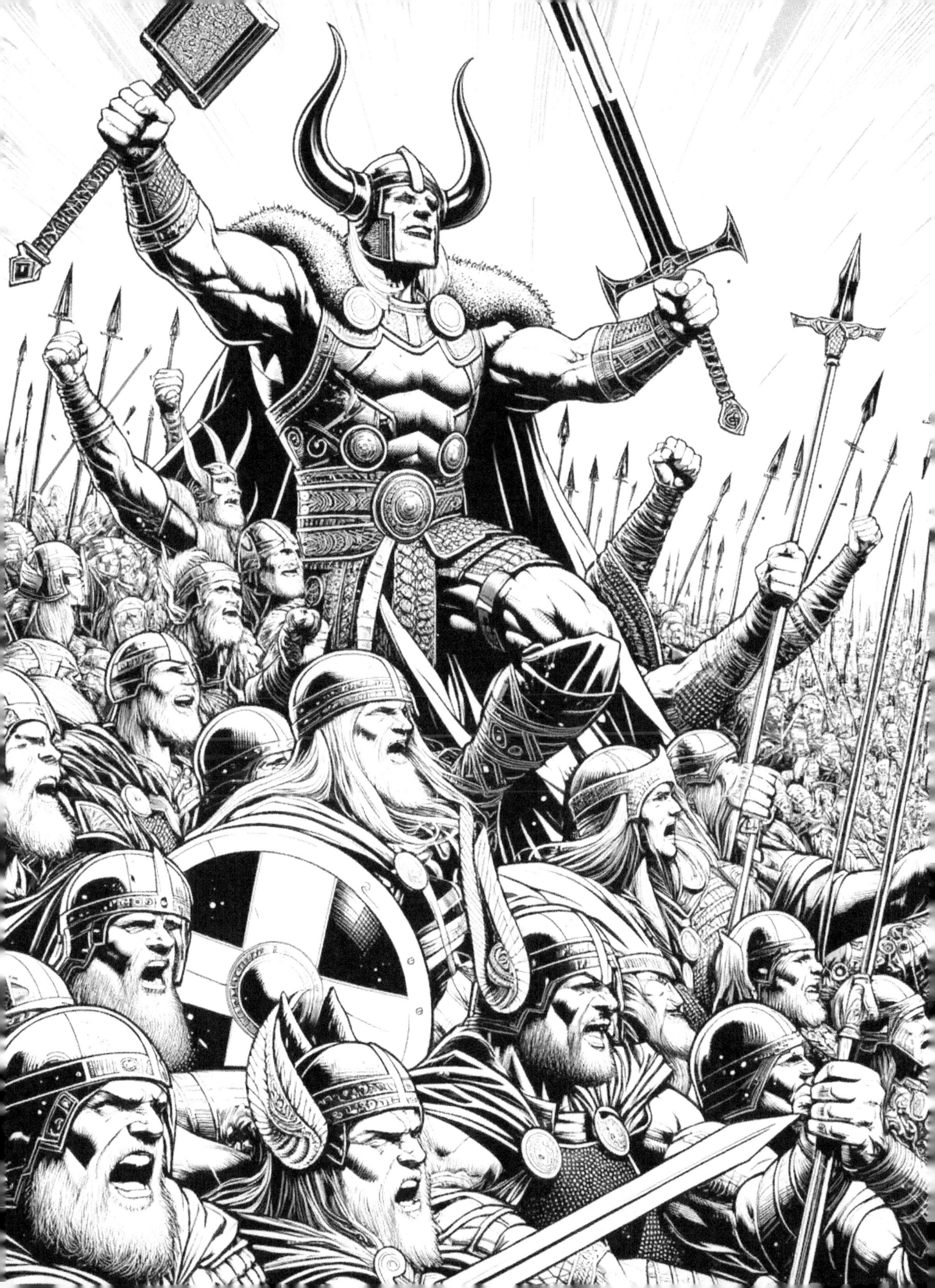

"Fenrir the Wolf"

The monstrous wolf, and son of Loki and Angrboda, the brother of Jormungandr and Hel. He is feared by the gods, for he is destined to kill Odin at Ragnarok, the doom of the gods. The gods try to bind him with various chains, but he breaks them all with his mighty strength. Only Gleipnir, the magic fetter made of six impossible things, can hold him. He bites off the hand of Tyr, the god of war, who dares to put it in his mouth as a pledge. He waits for the day of his final battle, when he will devour the All-father and meet his own death by Vidarr, Odin's son.

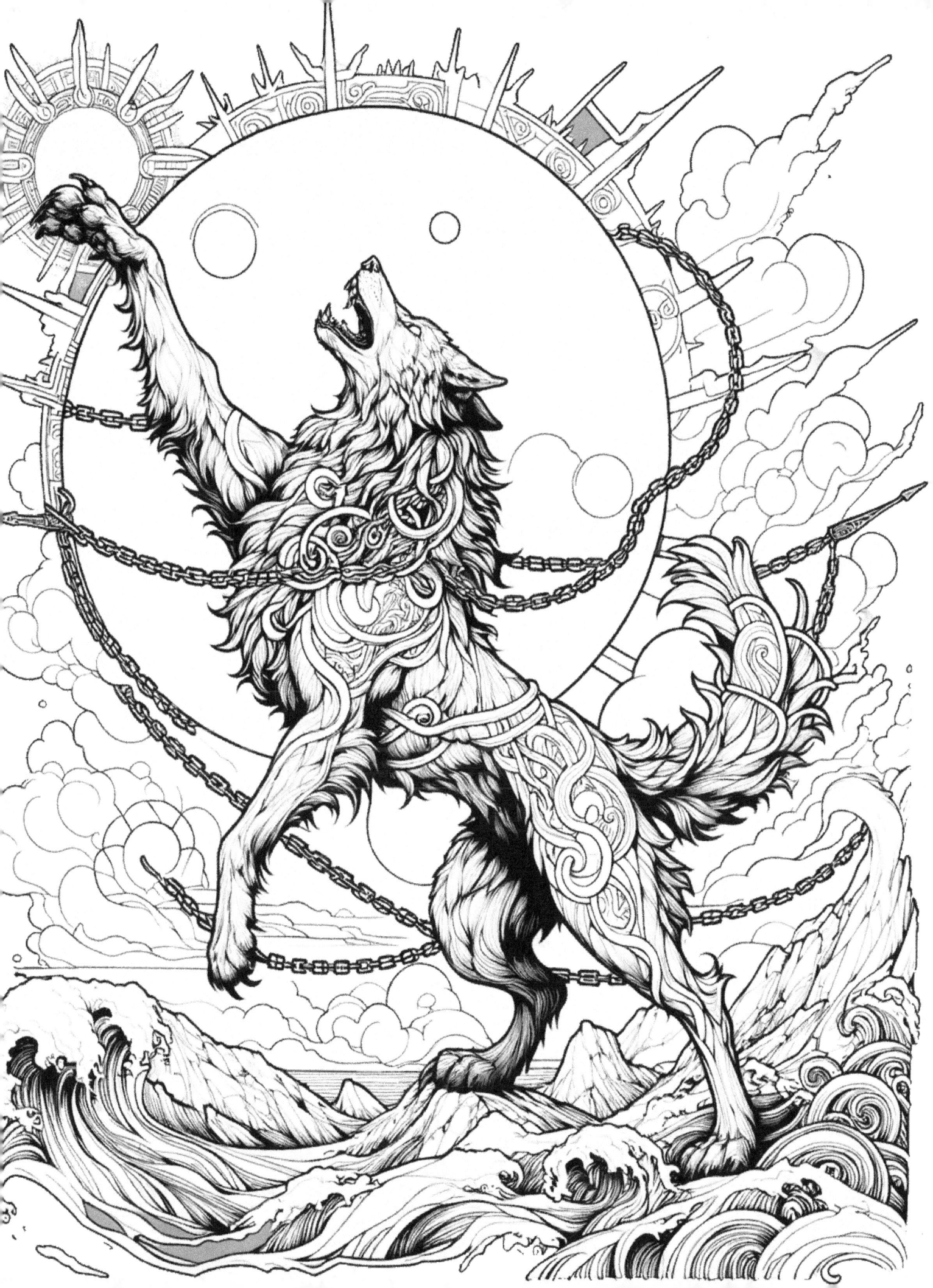

"The Demise of Odin and Fenrir"

Odin, the king of the gods, faced Fenrir, the giant wolf, at Ragnarok, the end of the world. Fenrir was so huge that his jaws could swallow the sky and the earth. Odin fought bravely, but he was no match for Fenrir's strength and ferocity. Fenrir bit Odin and tore him apart, killing him instantly. The other gods watched in horror as their leader fell. Odin's son, Vídarr, avenged his father by ripping Fenrir's mouth open and stabbing him in the heart. Fenrir died in agony, and the world was plunged into chaos.

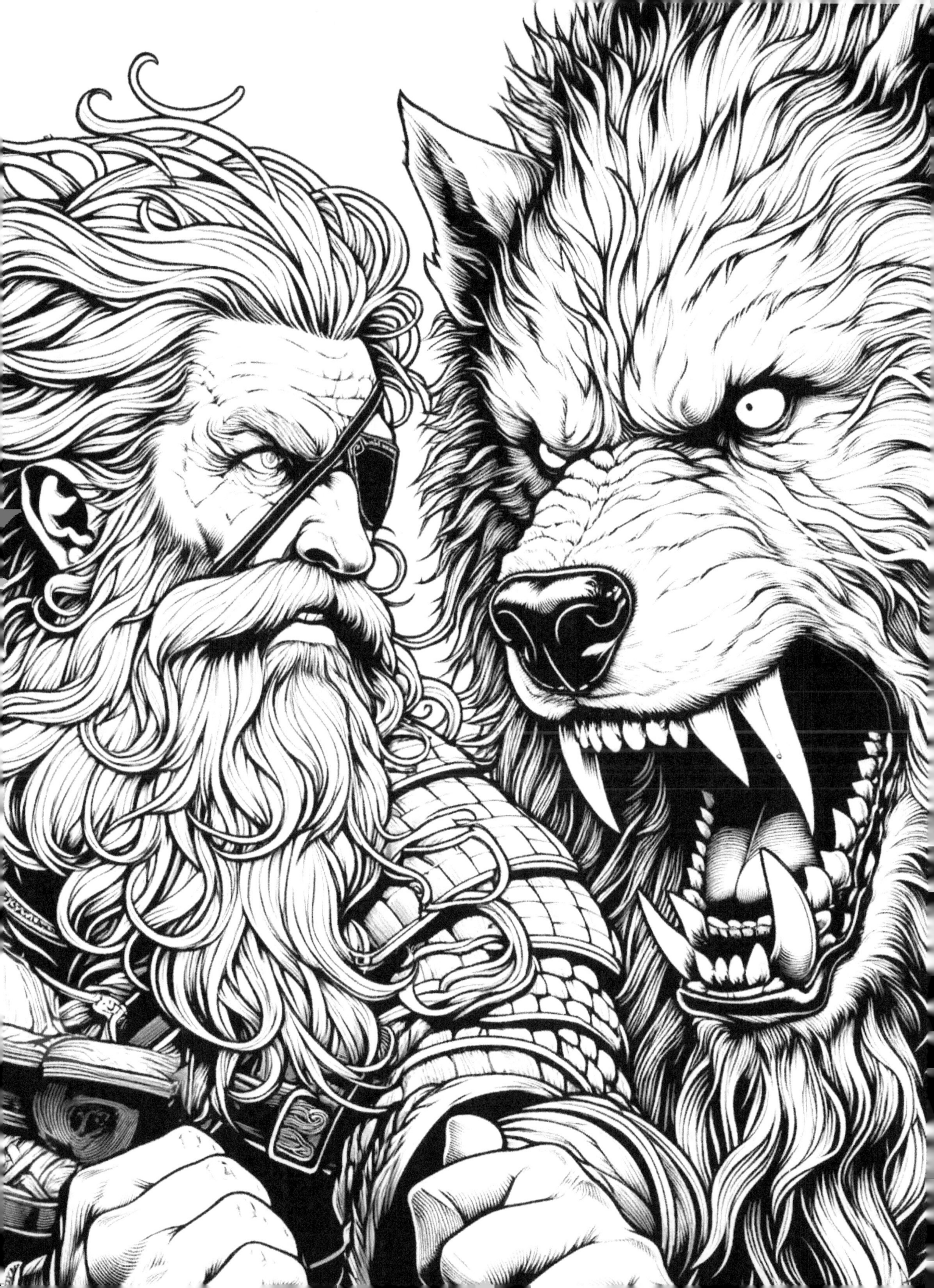

"The Unshackling of Loki"

After causing mischief and discord, Loki was bound by the gods as punishment. He is chained deep beneath the earth with a serpent poised above him, dripping venom. His faithful wife, Sigyn, stays by his side, catching the poison in a bowl, sparing him agony. However, when she must empty the bowl, the venom strikes Loki, causing him to writhe in pain, his convulsions were believed to cause earthquakes. As Ragnarok approaches, Loki breaks free from his chains, emerging embittered and vengeful. This moment signifies his transformation from a trickster to a harbinger of the end, joining forces against the gods in the final battle.

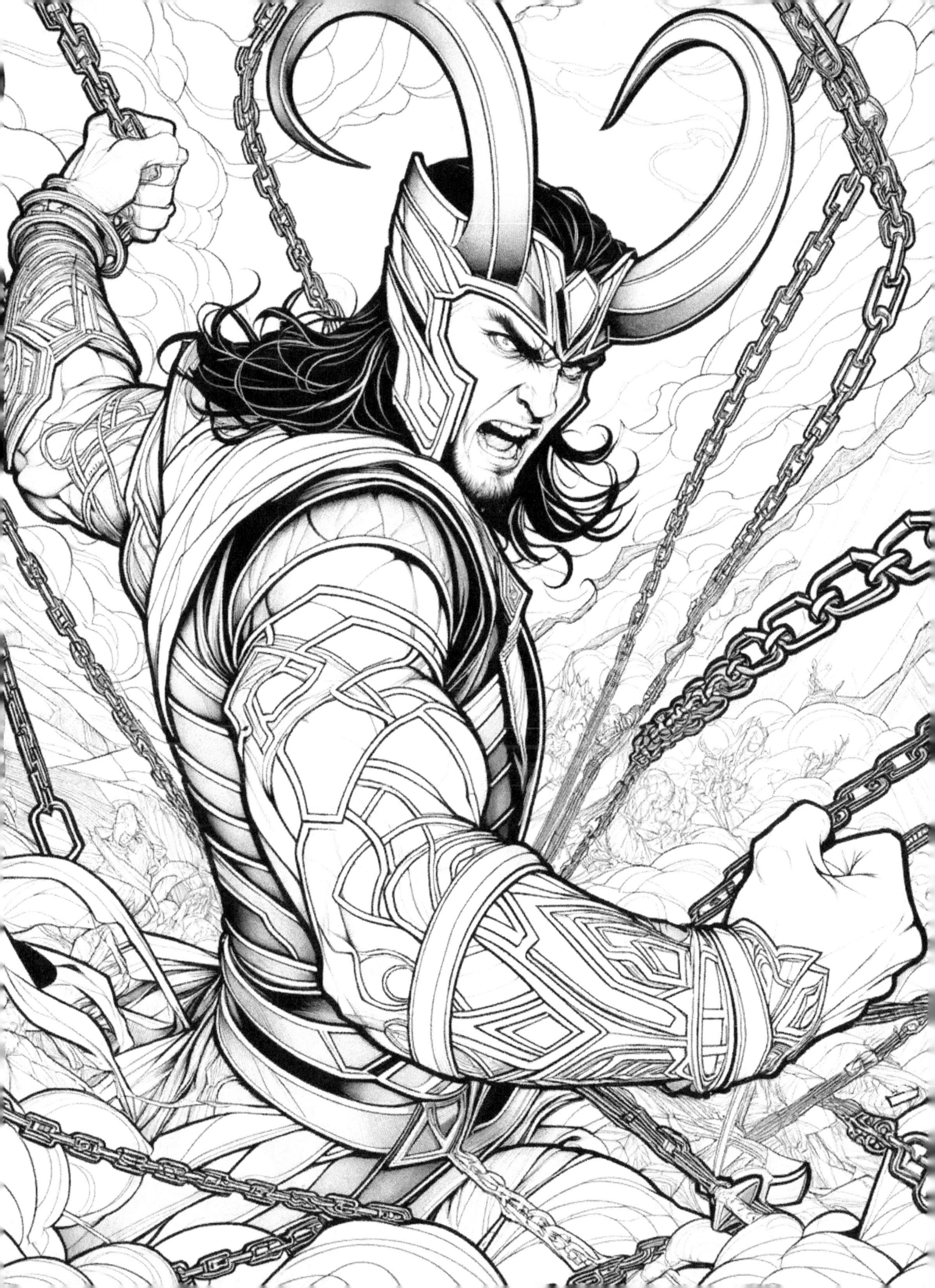

"Naglfar: The Ship of the Dead"

A colossal vessel made entirely from the fingernails and toenails of the dead. This macabre ship, lurking in the dark waters of the underworld, is a harbinger of chaos and destruction. As Ragnarok approaches, Naglfar breaks free, captained by the giant Hrym and carrying legions of the dead towards the battlefield. Its very appearance signifies the beginning of the end, as it ferries these sinister forces to join the final battle against the gods. Naglfar embodies the culmination of all fears and horrors, a grim testament to the power of death and decay.

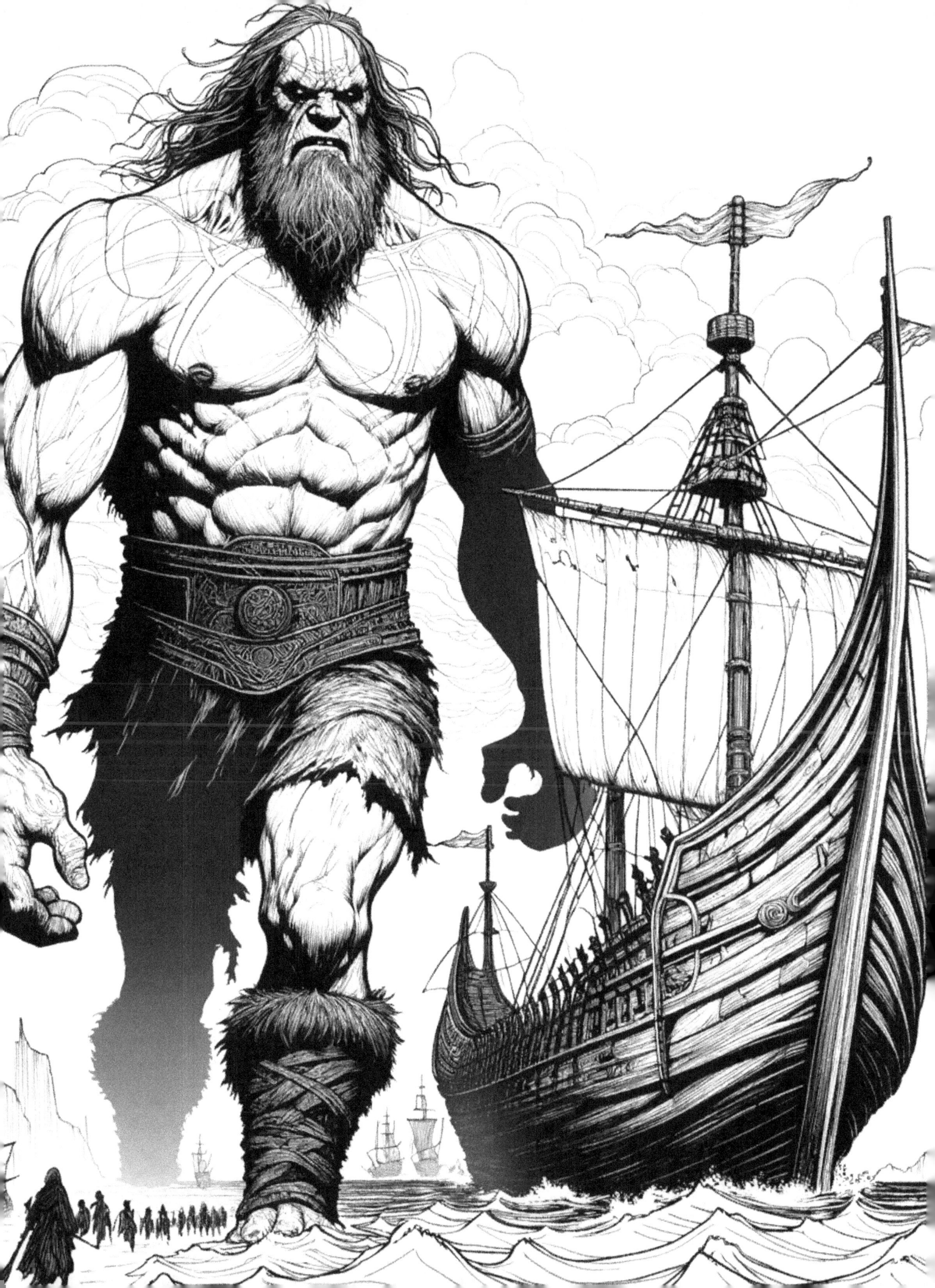

"Yggdrasil: The World Tree"

The immense cosmic tree that connects the Nine Realms in Norse mythology, suffers greatly. As the cataclysmic events unfold, Yggdrasil shakes and trembles, signifying the collapse of the old order. The tree withstands immense stress as the realms are engulfed in conflict, with gods and giants clashing in a final battle. Fire engulfs its branches, and the serpent Jormungandr's violent thrashing at its roots further damages it. Despite this turmoil, Yggdrasil does not perish but remains standing, enduring as a symbol of resilience and the enduring cycle of life, death, and rebirth in the universe.

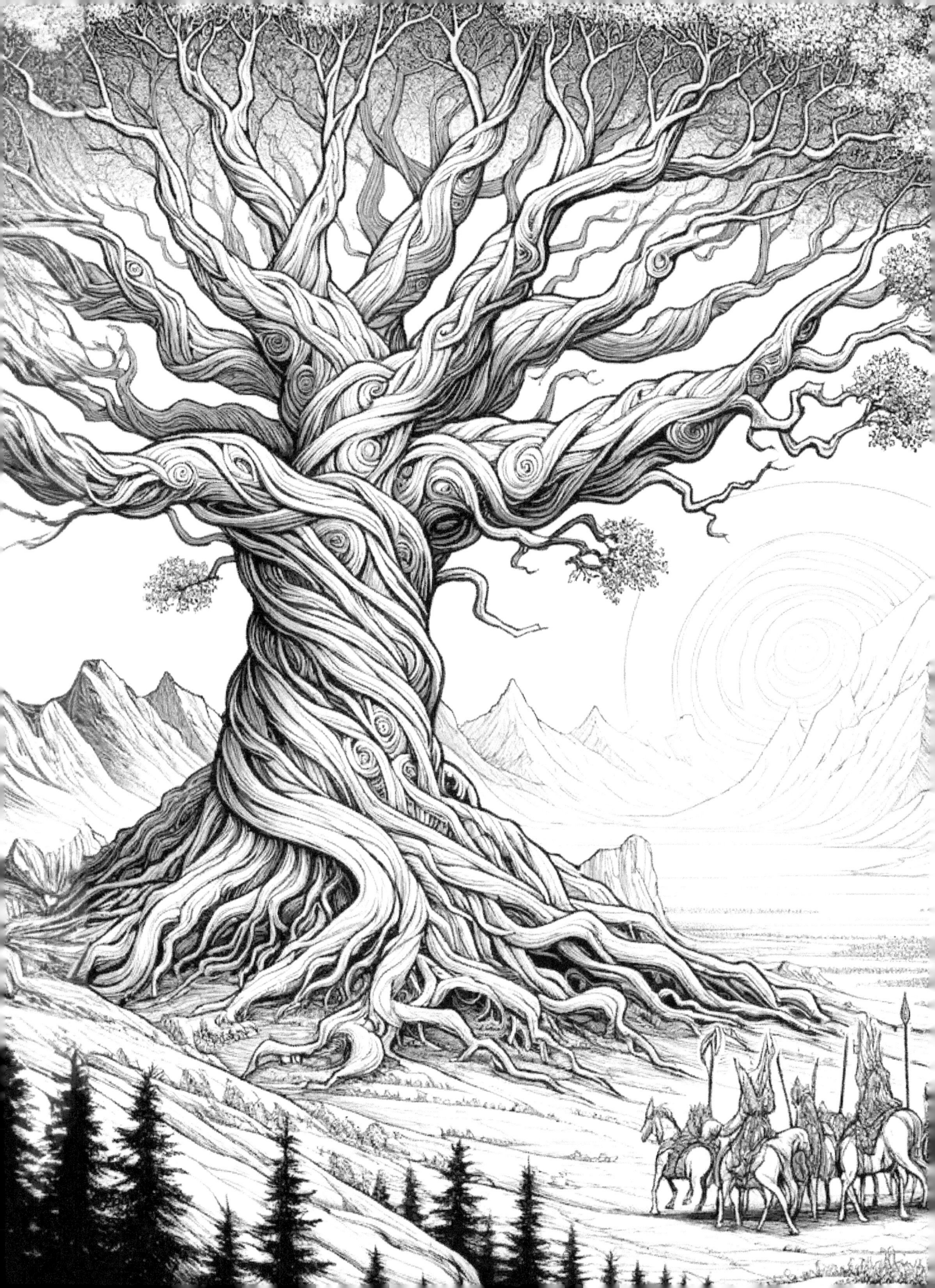

"Bifrost"

The Rainbow Bridge arched gracefully between realms, a shimmering kaleidoscope connecting Asgard, the realm of the gods, to Midgard, the world of humans. Its radiant hues spanned the spectrum, from the fiery reds of Muspelheim to the icy blues of Jotunheim. Guarded by Heimdall, the vigilant watchman, it resonated with harmonious vibrations. Bifrost was both a celestial pathway and a fragile link, foretelling Ragnarok's fiery end. As mortals glimpsed its beauty, they knew it was a bridge to realms beyond, a bridge of destiny, where gods and humans might meet and where fate's threads converged.

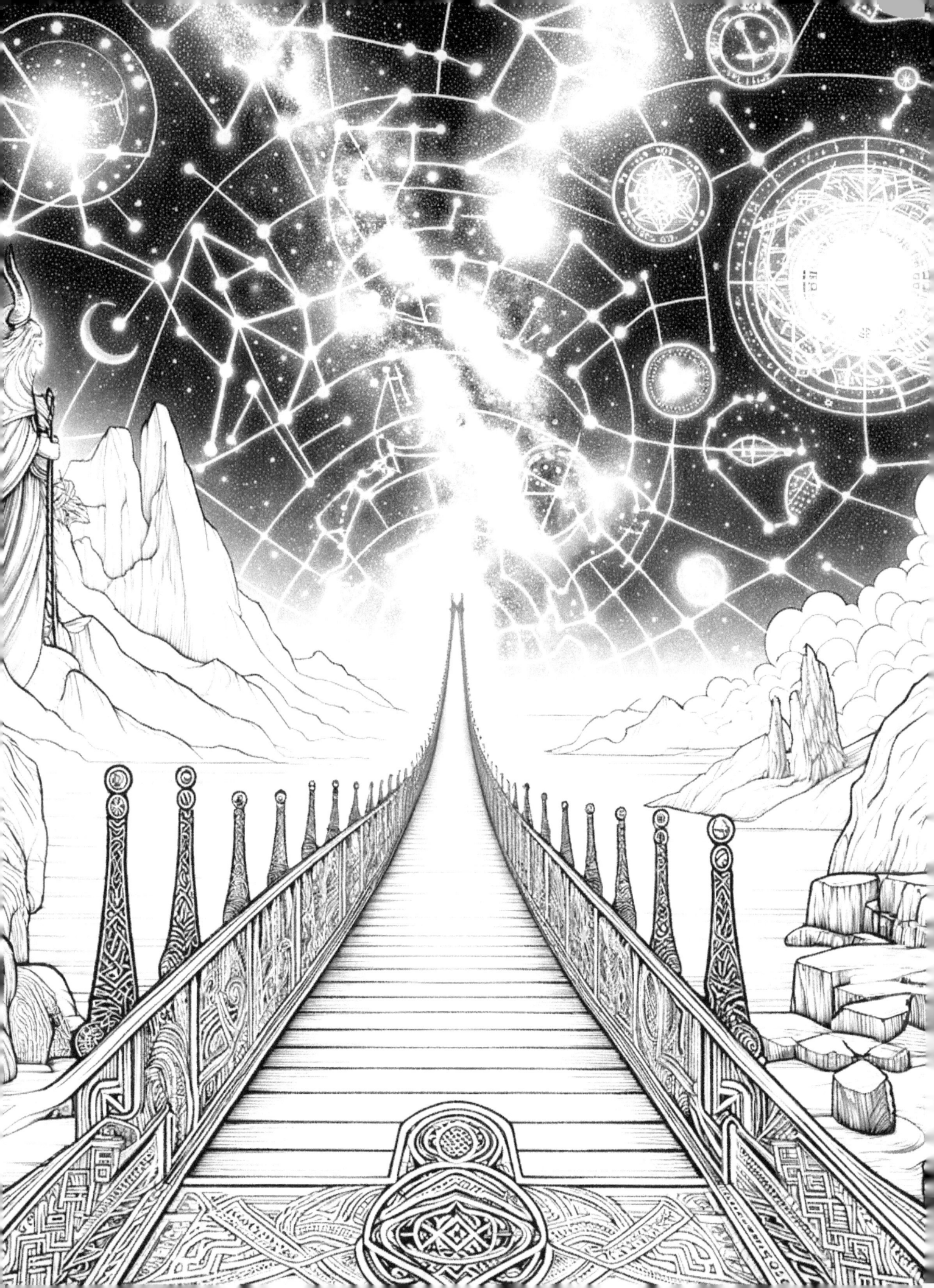

"The Guardian: Heimdall"

The watchman of the gods is a vigilant guardian stationed at Bifrost, the rainbow bridge to Asgard. With extraordinary senses, he hears grass growing and sees for a hundred leagues, ever alert to dangers threatening the realm of the gods. Heimdall possesses the resounding horn, Gjallarhorn, which he is destined to blow at the onset of Ragnarok, signaling the gods to battle. In this apocalyptic war, he confronts and slays Loki but is himself mortally wounded. Heimdall's demise, like that of many gods during Ragnarok, marks the end of an era and the transition to a new cosmic cycle.

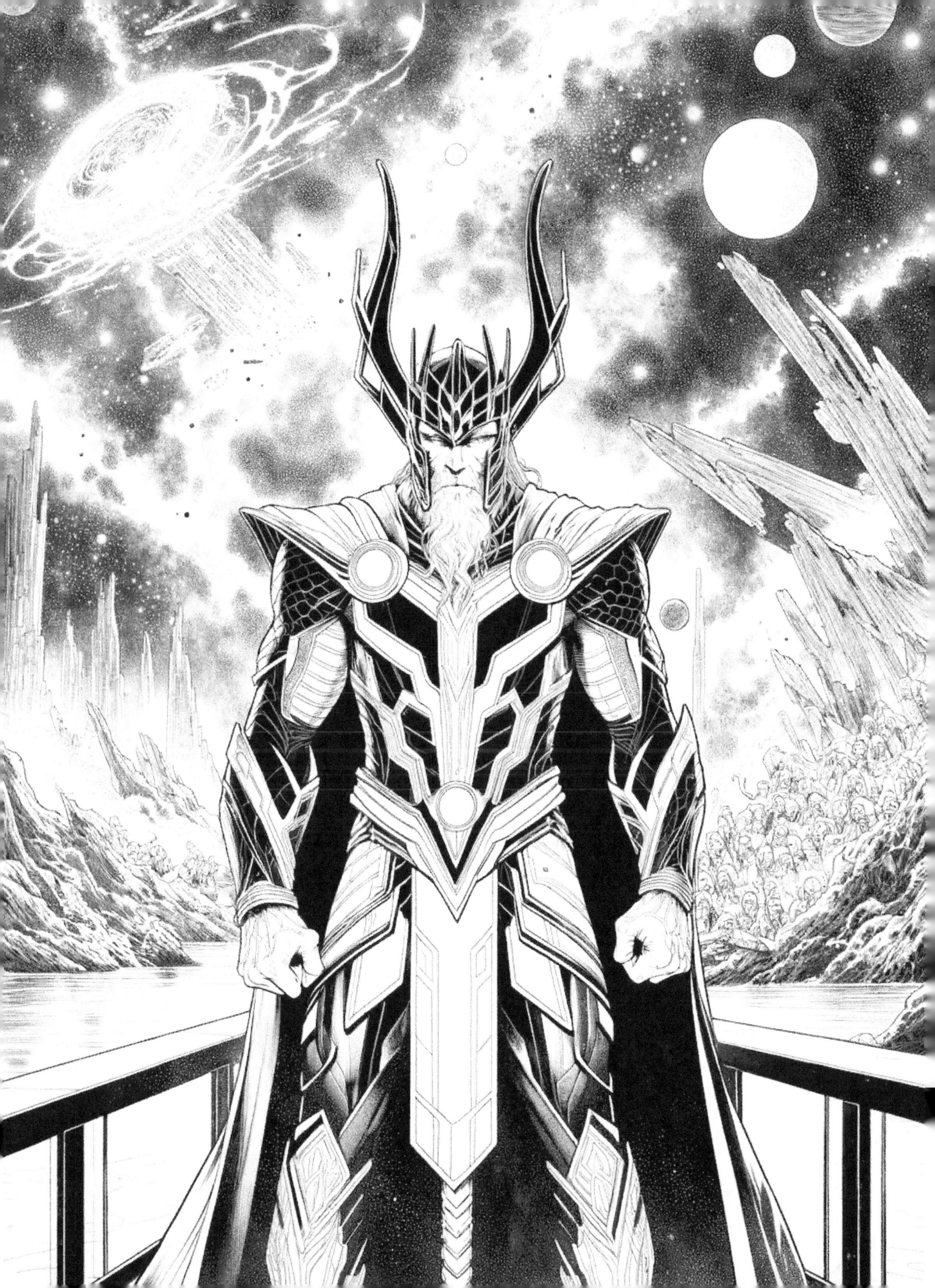

"The Destruction of Bifrost"

The cataclysmic event loomed, casting an ominous shadow over the celestial bridge. As the forces of chaos and destruction surged, Bifrost quivered under the pressure. Its vibrant hues dimmed, fading from the heavens as if the very colors wept for their impending fate. A deafening roar filled the air, drowning the once-harmonious resonance. The bridge buckled and fractured, ethereal fragments scattering like stardust. Flames and ice clashed, consuming Bifrost's splendor, and the bridge that had once united realms now crumbled, leaving a void in the cosmic tapestry.

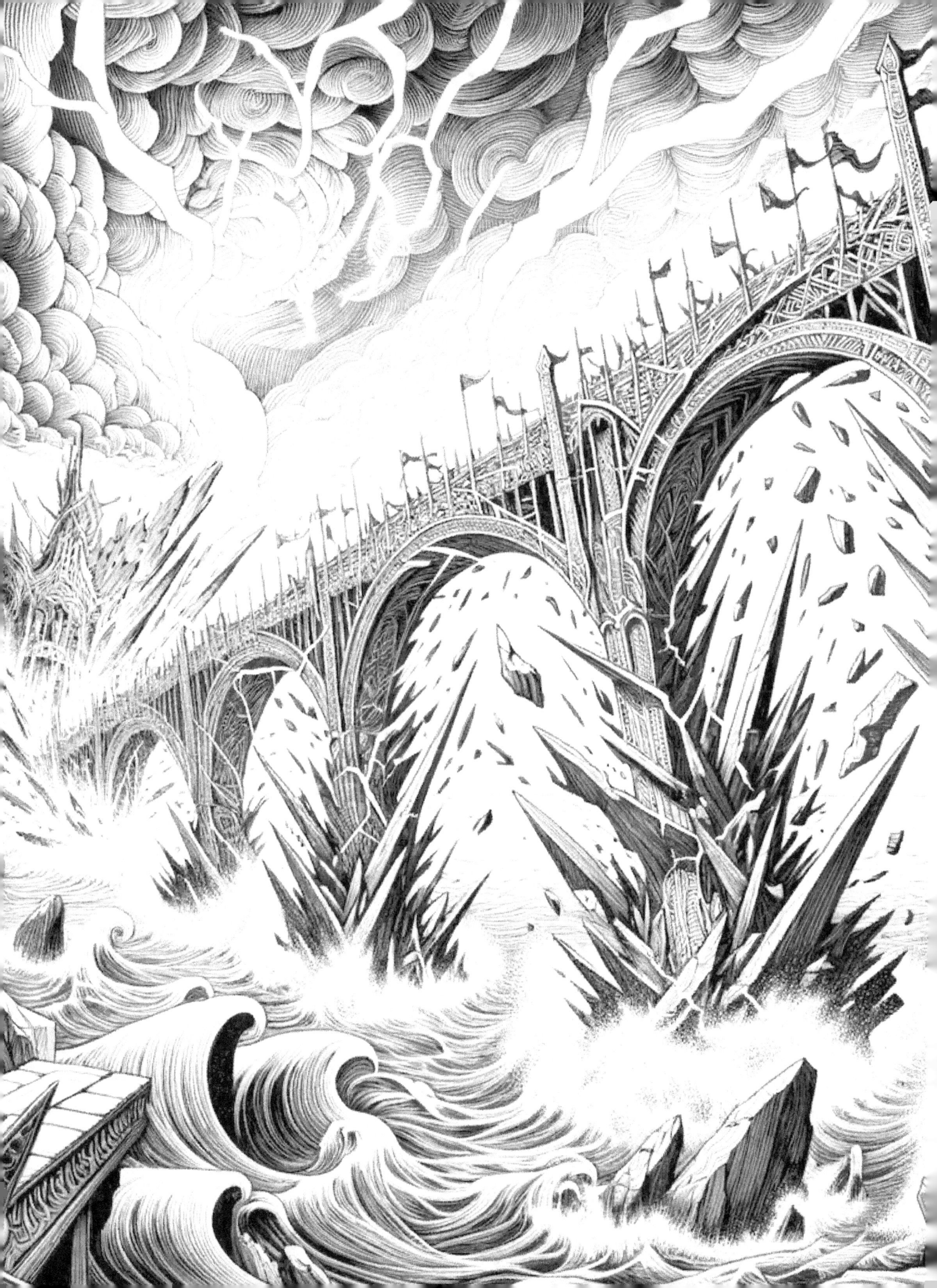

"Jormungandr, The World Serpent"

The World Serpent encircles Midgard, the human world, biting its own tail. Born to Loki and the giantess Angrboda, Jormungandr symbolizes the boundaries of the world and the perpetual cycle of life and death. This immense serpent maintains the world's balance by holding the seas in place. During Ragnarok, Jormungandr releases its tail, causing cataclysmic upheavals. It surfaces from the ocean, spewing venom and causing widespread destruction. In a climactic battle, Jormungandr faces its archenemy, Thor. Thor slays the serpent but succumbs to its poisonous breath, marking their mutual demise and the fulfillment of their destiny.

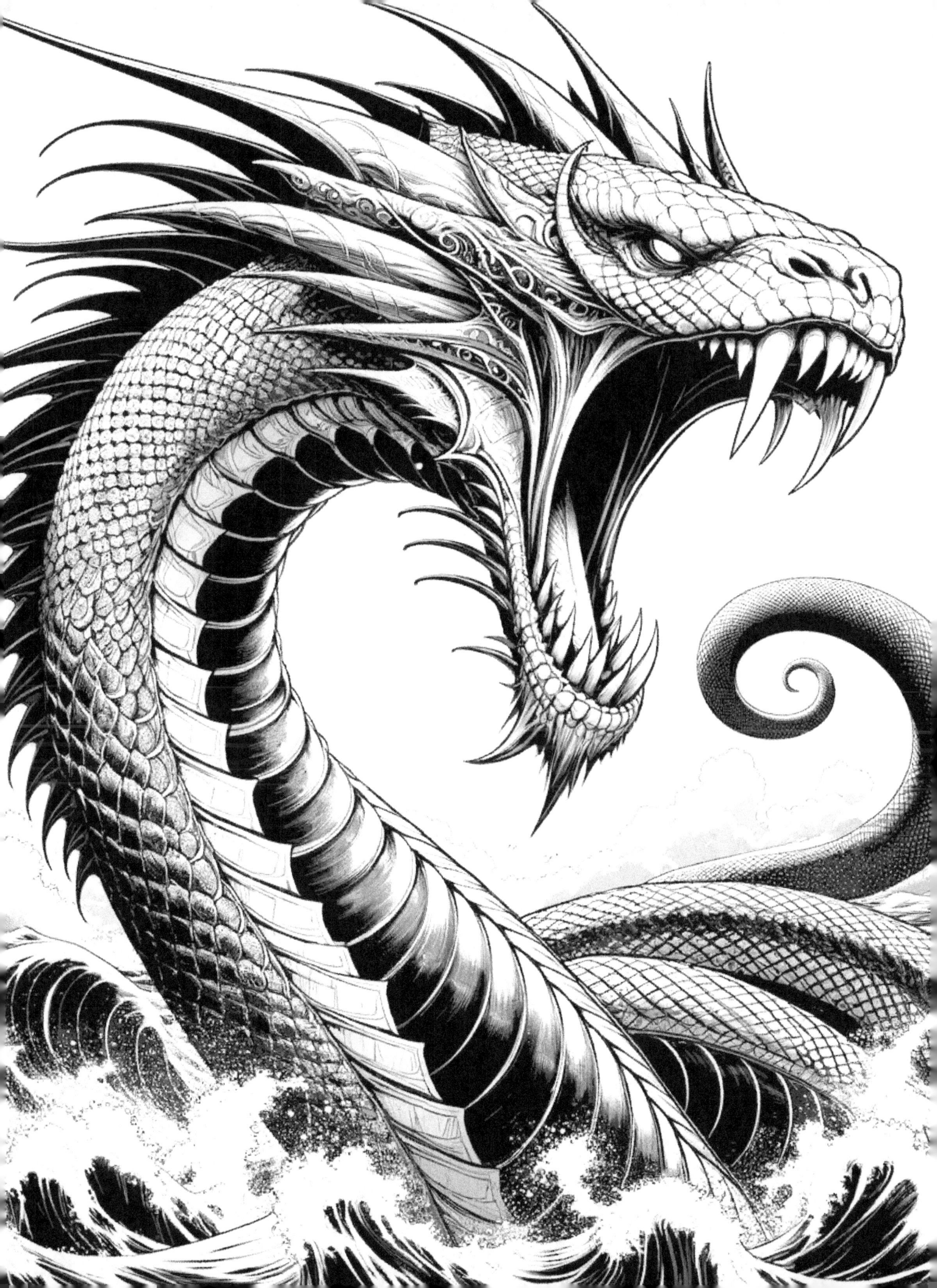

"Midgard: The Realm of Humanity"

The middle realm, home to humanity, nestled securely between the realms of the gods and giants. This earthly domain, encircled by the colossal serpent Jormungandr, is a vibrant land of mountains, forests, and seas, bustling with human life and activity. It's connected to Asgard, the realm of the gods, via Bifrost, the rainbow bridge. Midgard represents the mortal experience, a place of struggle, bravery, and the pursuit of honor. It is a crucial battlefield during Ragnarok, where gods and mortals alike fight against chaos and destruction, highlighting the interwoven fate of all the realms.

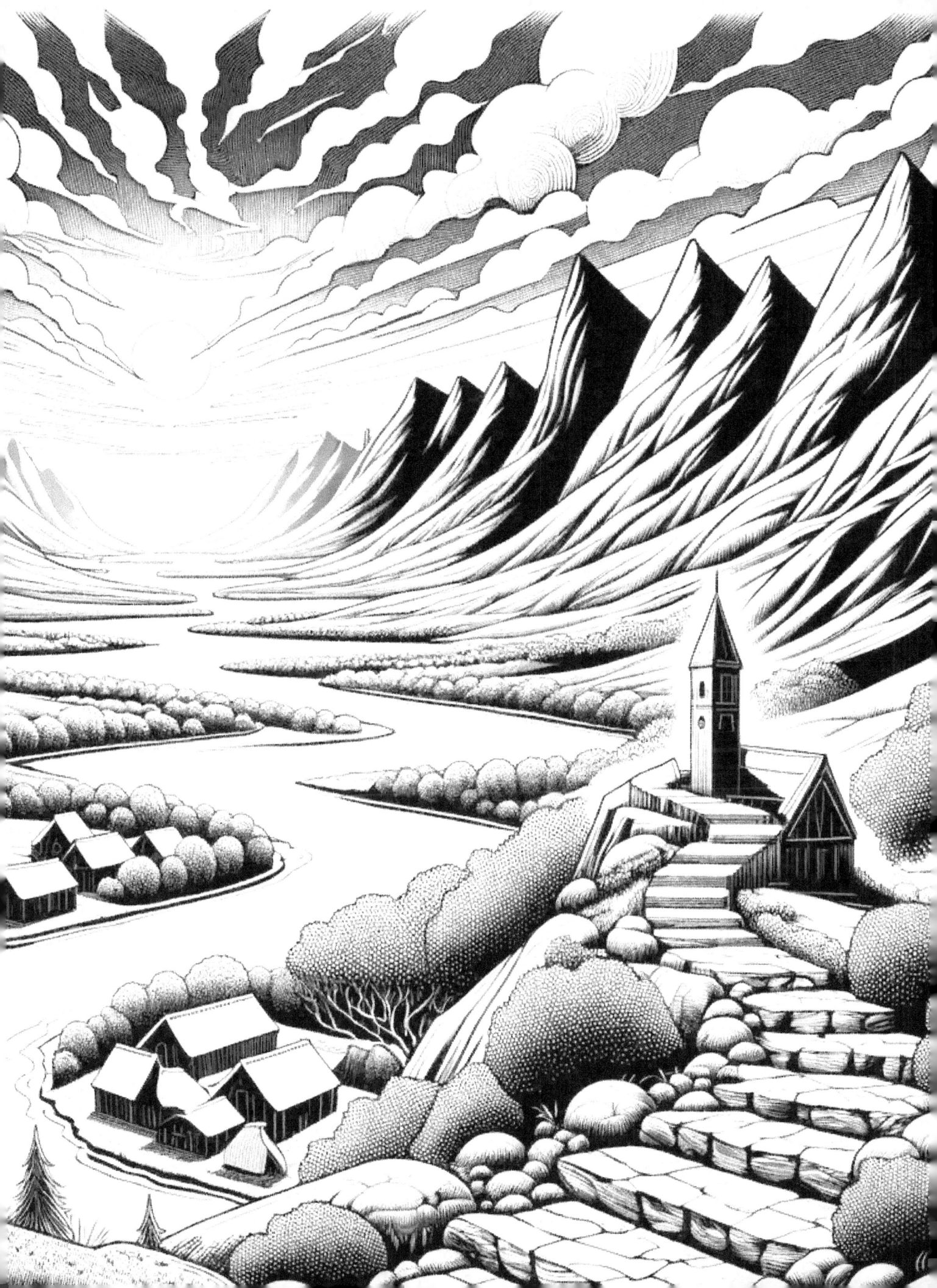

"Thor: God of Thunder"

A formidable figure in Norse mythology, known for his immense strength and heroic deeds. Son of Odin and Fjorgyn, he wields Mjolnir, his mighty hammer, capable of leveling mountains. With his chariot pulled by two goats, Thor controls the skies, manifesting thunder and lightning. A protector of Asgard and Midgard, he embodies physical prowess and valor. Renowned for battling giants, Thor's exploits showcase his bravery and resilience. At Ragnarok, he faces his ultimate challenge against Jormungandr, triumphing over the serpent but succumbing to its venom, symbolizing the heroic yet mortal nature of the gods.

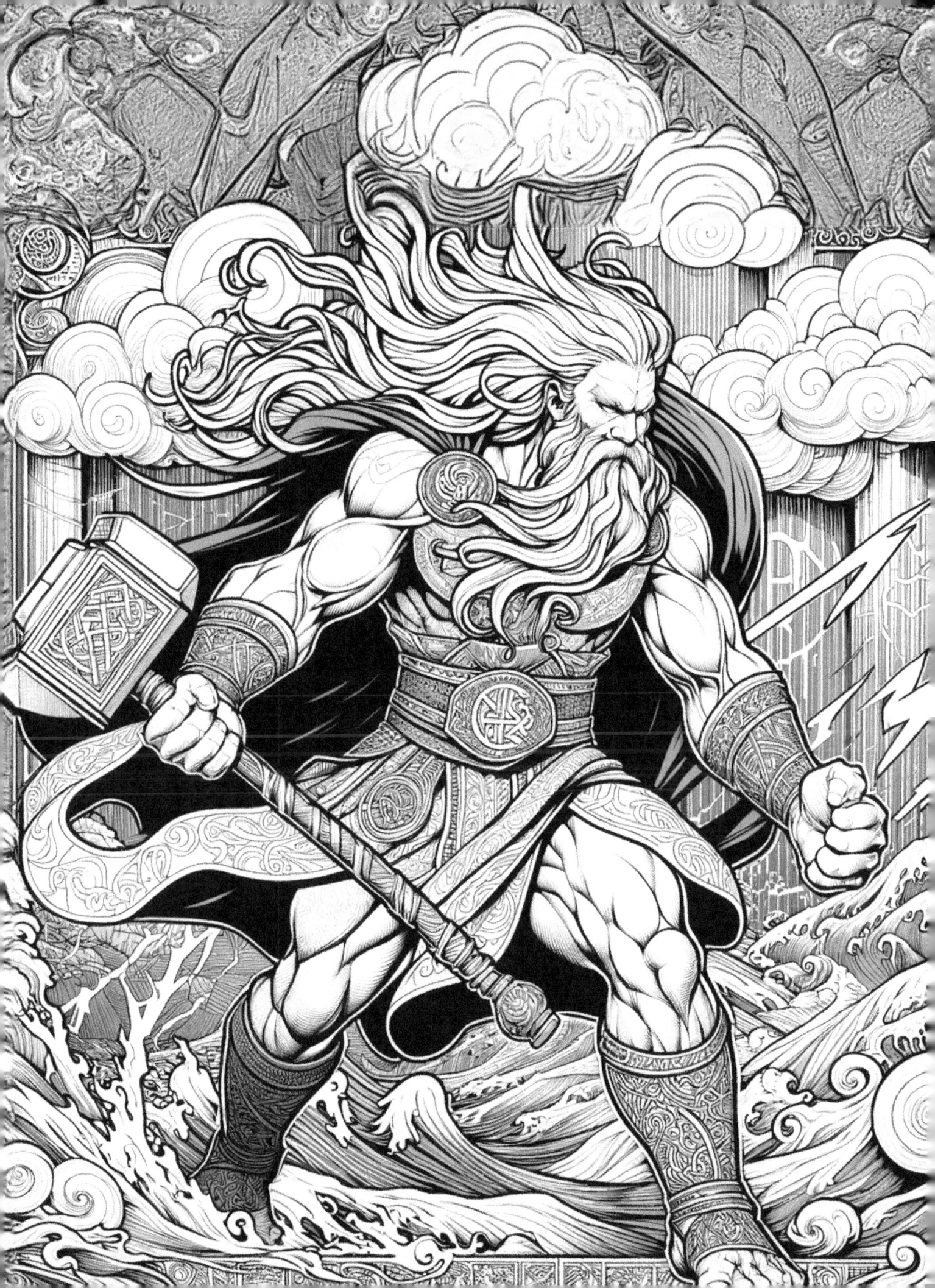

"Sif"

A radiant goddess, celebrated for her long, golden hair which shimmered like fields of ripe wheat. As the wife of Thor, the thunder god, she embodied the nurturing aspect of fertility, her tresses symbolizing the bountiful harvest. Sif's presence graced the agrarian world, ensuring abundant crops and prosperity for mortals. Her story also involves the trickster Loki, who once cut off her hair, causing strife until he replaced it with even more exquisite locks of gold, crafted by the skilled dwarves of Nidavellir. Sif remains an embodiment of beauty, fertility, and the essential connection between the divine and earthly realms.

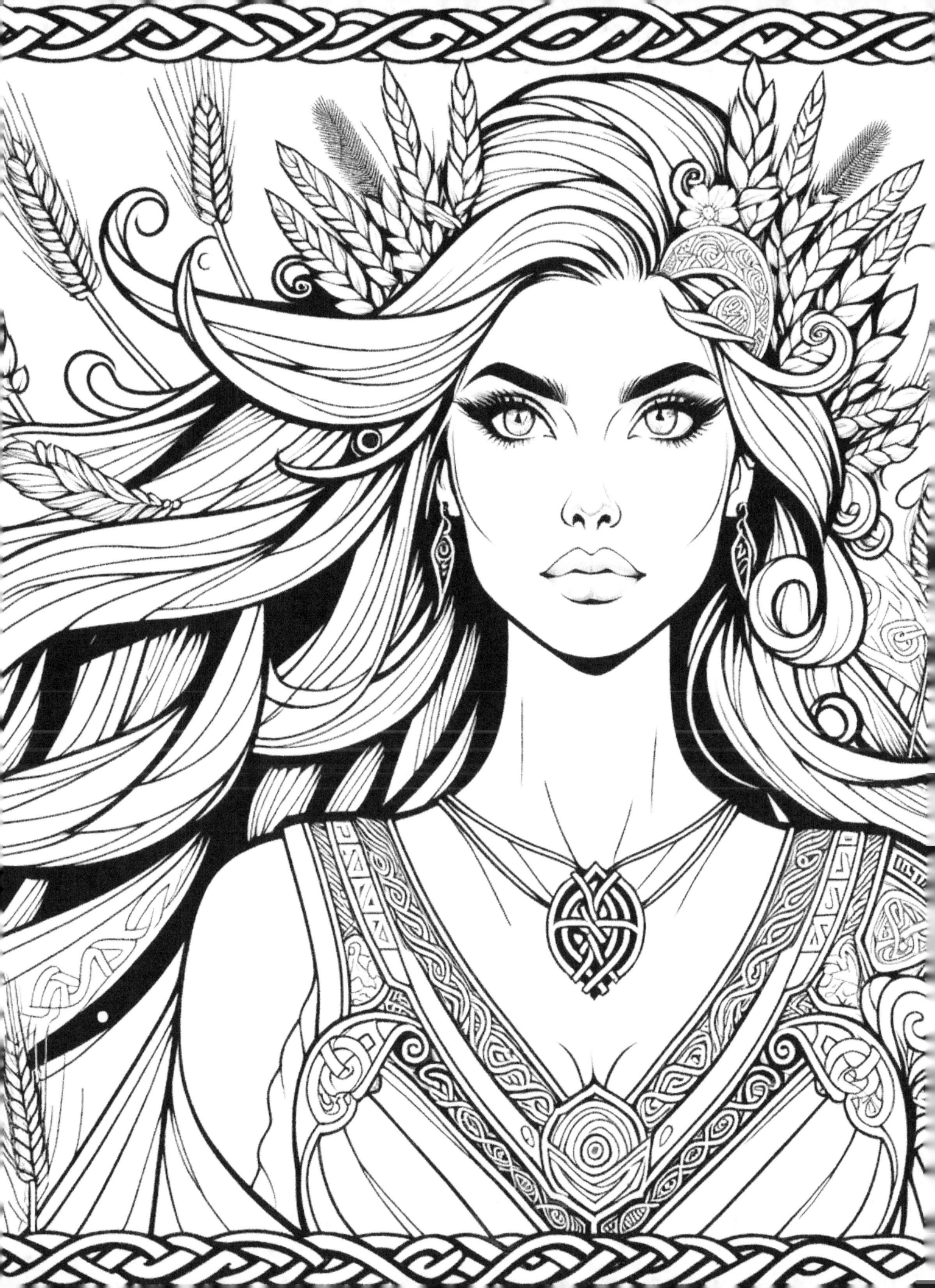

"Thunders End"

At Ragnarok, Thor, the god of thunder, confronts his arch-nemesis, Jormungandr, the World Serpent. As Jormungandr releases its tail, signaling the end, it emerges from the ocean, unleashing chaos. Thor, wielding his mighty hammer Mjolnir, engages in a titanic battle with the serpent. Amidst thunder and lightning, he strikes Jormungandr, dealing a fatal blow. However, the victory is bittersweet. Thor, victorious, walks nine steps before succumbing to the serpent's venomous breath. This epic confrontation between the god of thunder and the colossal serpent marks their mutual demise.

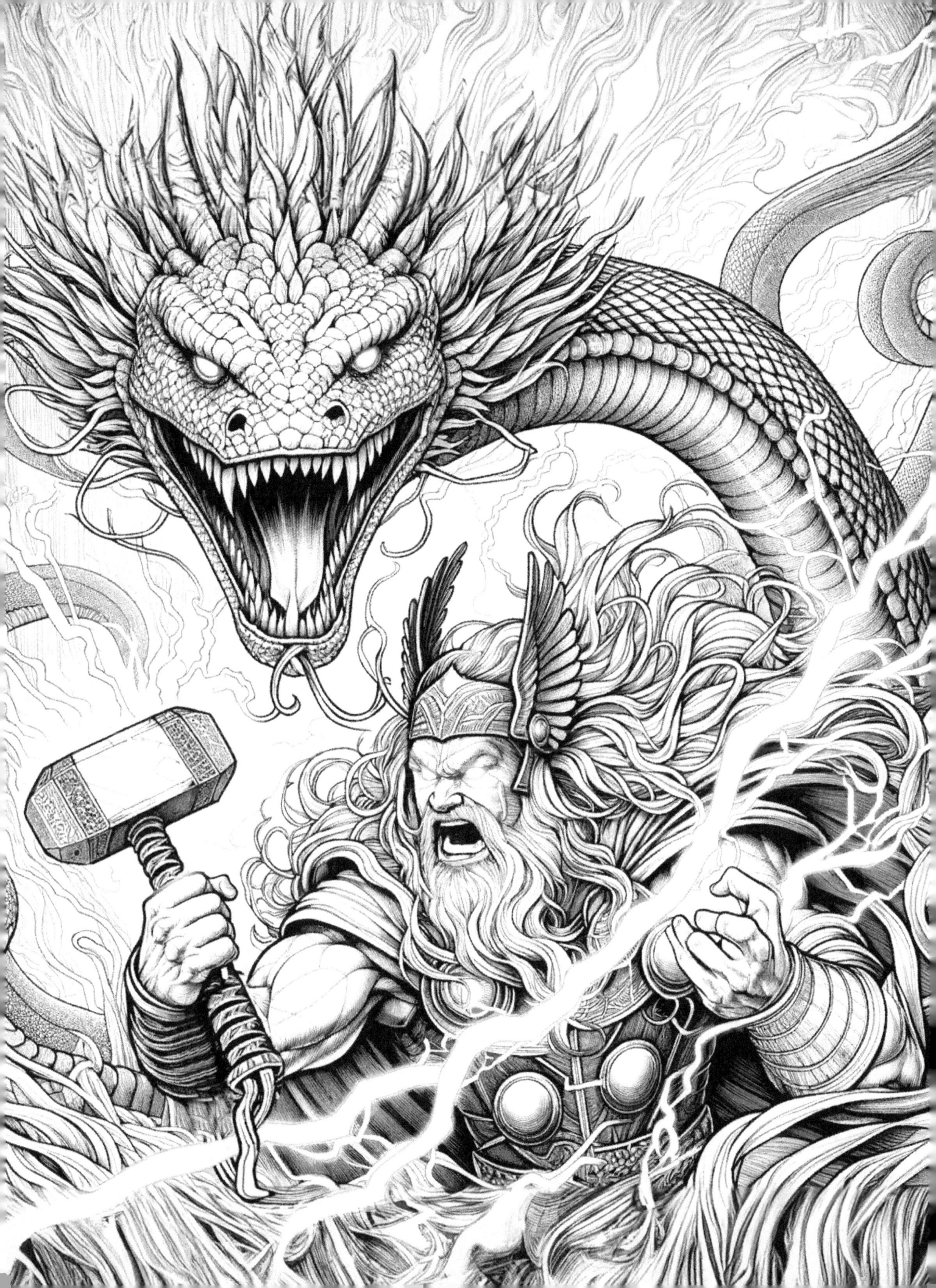

"The Realm of Jotunheim"

The rugged and untamed realm of the giants, a land of mountains, dense forests, and dark winters. It lies beyond the world of gods and men, separated by the river Iving, a boundary that few dare to cross. The giants, known as Jotunn or Jotnar, are beings of immense power and ancient wisdom, often at odds with the gods of Asgard. Their land is one of primal wilderness, where the raw forces of nature reign supreme. Jotunheim's harsh landscape and its formidable inhabitants embody the timeless struggle between the structured world of the gods and the untamed elemental chaos.

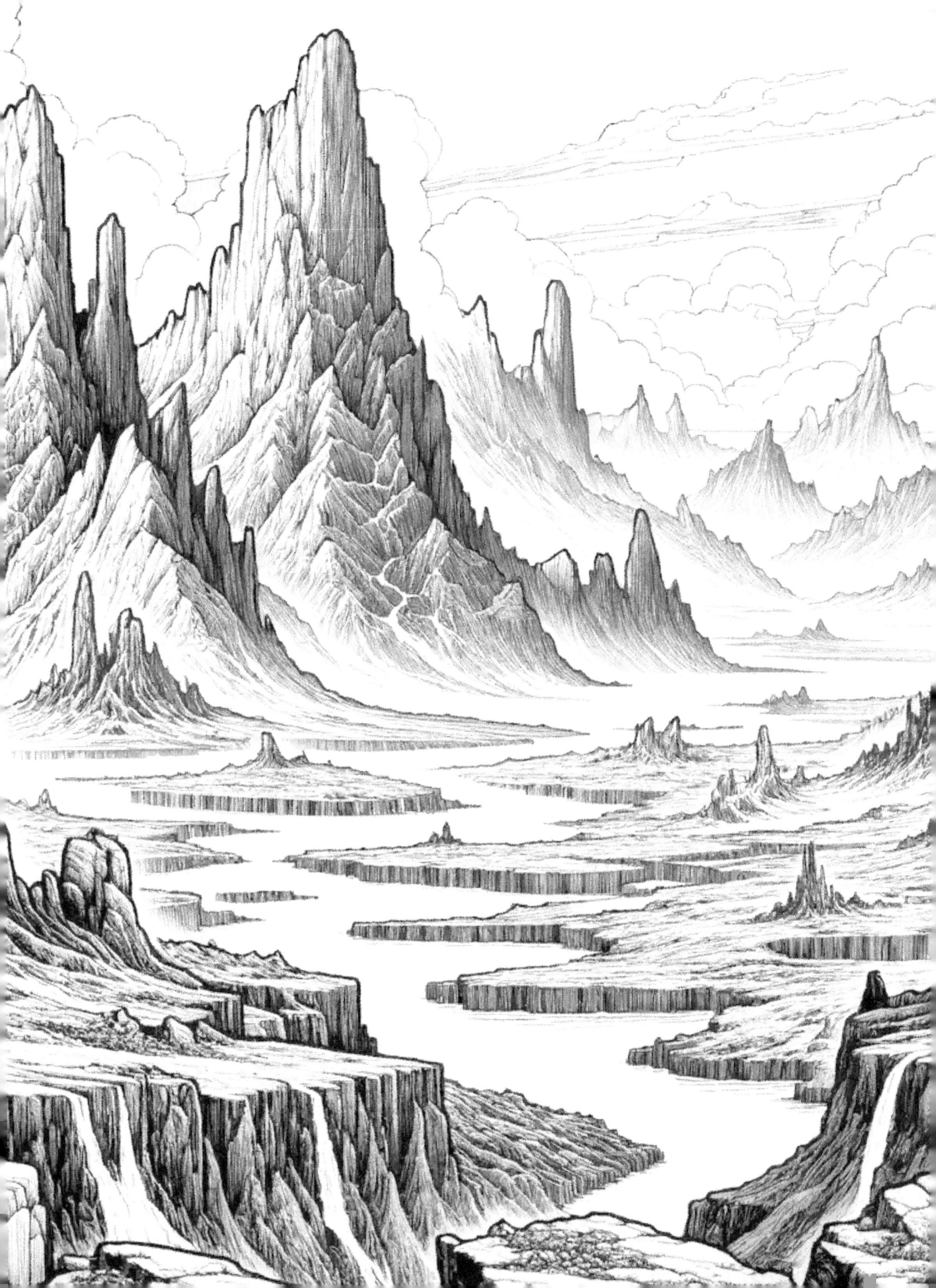

"The Jotunn"

A race of giants inhabiting Jotunheim, a realm of raw, untamed wilderness. These beings are formidable and diverse, ranging from the frost giants of icy wastes to the mountain giants of rocky landscapes. Often portrayed as adversaries of the gods, the Jotunn embody the forces of nature and chaos, challenging the order of Asgard. Some, like Loki, are known for their cunning and shape-shifting abilities. Despite their often contentious relationship with the gods.

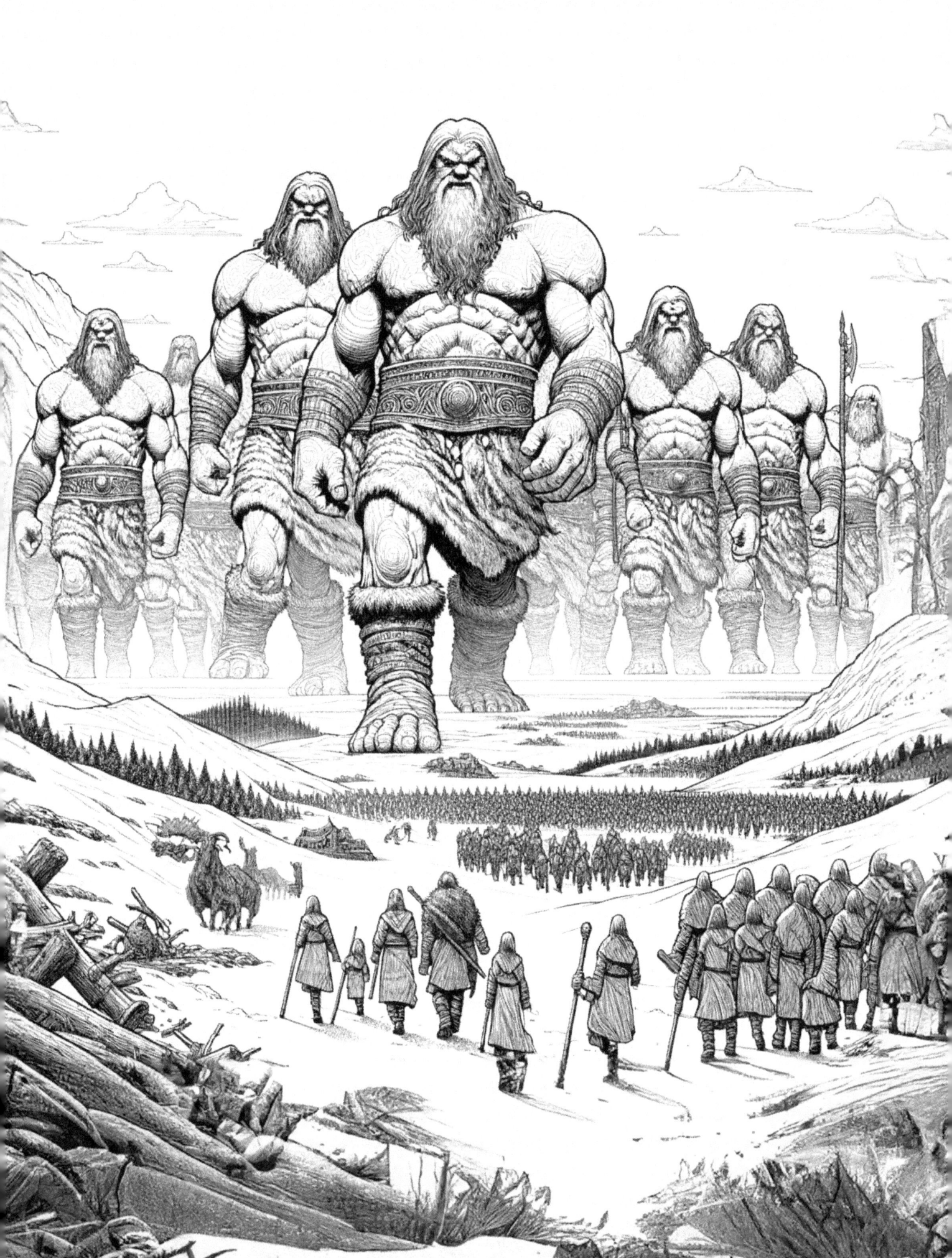

"The Realm of Niflheim"

"The World of Mist", is a realm of ice, frost, and fog, lying at the universe's fringes. It's a desolate, perpetually cold land, where rivers of ice flow and chilling winds never cease. Niflheim is ruled by Hel, the daughter of Loki, and serves as the final destination for those who don't die a heroic or notable death. This shadowy, mist-enshrouded world symbolizes the inhospitable and lifeless aspects of the cosmos. It contrasts sharply with the fiery realm of Muspelheim.

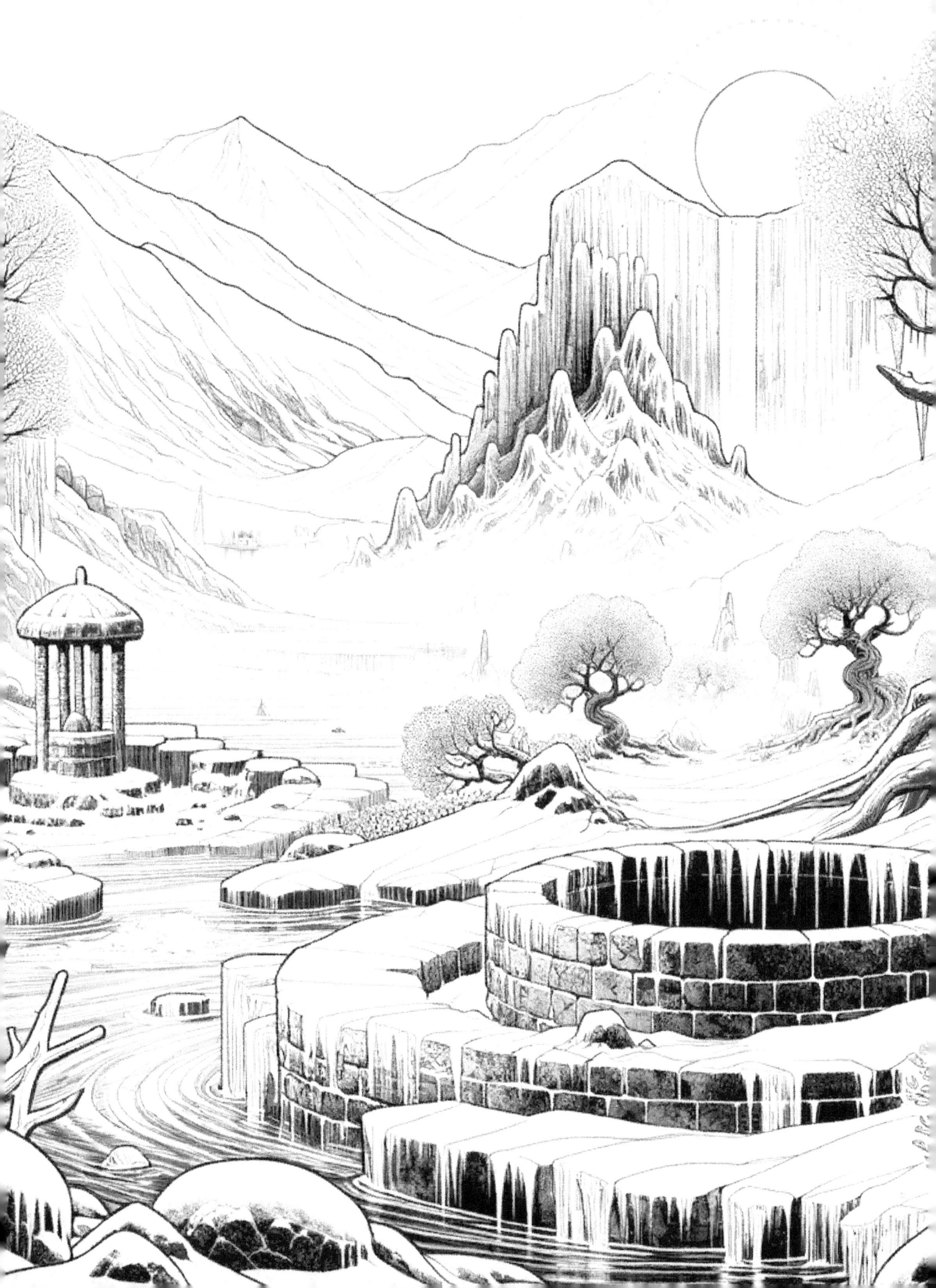

"Hel, Goddess of the Underworld"

Ruling over the eponymous realm, Helheim. A daughter of Loki, she is depicted as a figure of dual nature, often shown as half alive and half dead, symbolizing the boundary between life and death. Helheim, her domain, is the final resting place for those who don't die in battle. Her appearance is daunting, reflecting her role as the overseer of the dead. Despite her grim duties, Hel maintains order in her realm, ensuring that the deceased are adequately cared for. She embodies the inevitability of death and the solemn dignity that accompanies it.

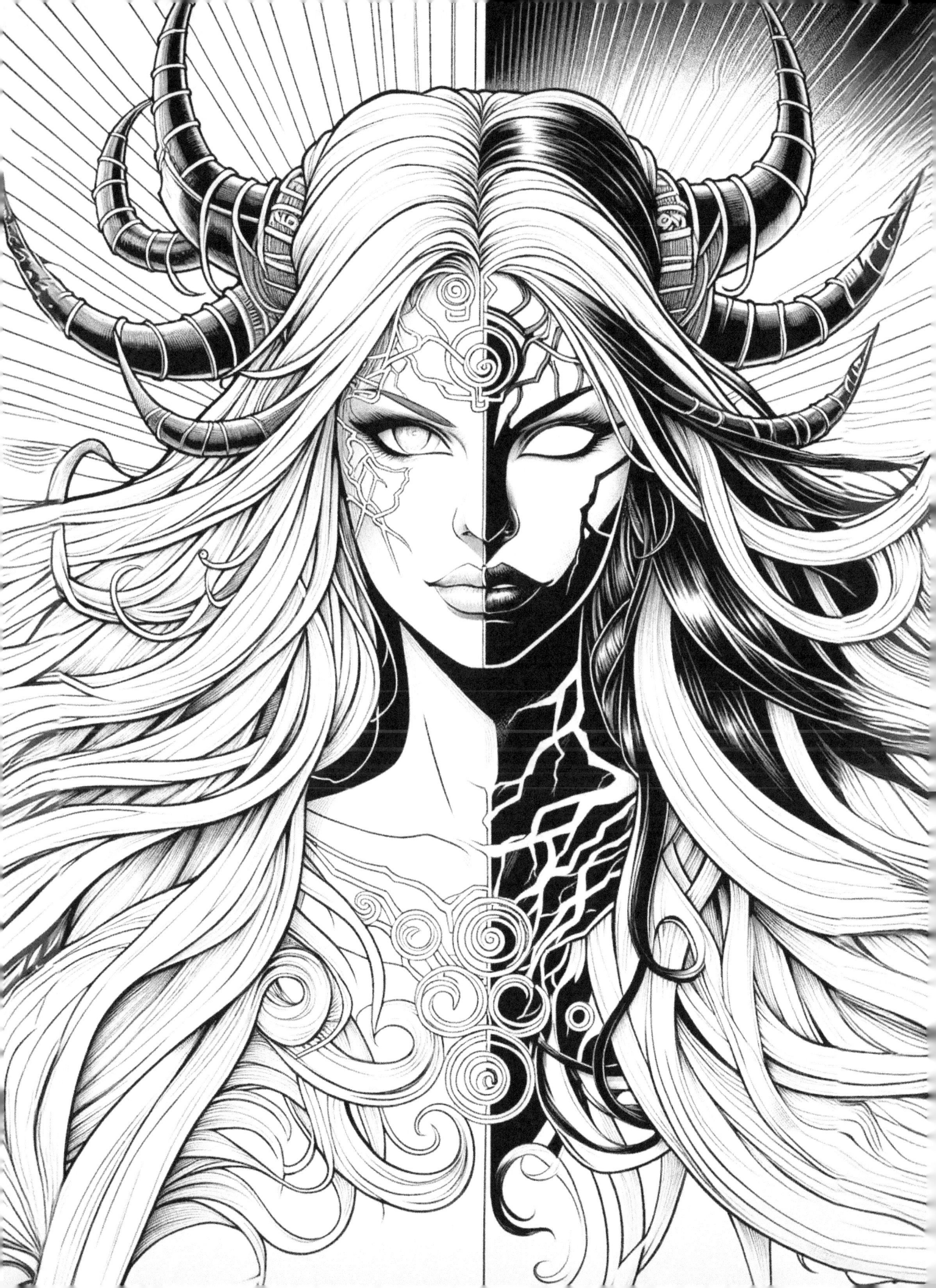

"The Underworld - Helheim"

The somber, mist-shrouded realm of the dead, situated within Niflheim, the world of cold and mist. Ruled by the goddess Hel, a daughter of Loki, it's the final resting place for those who don't die heroically in battle. Contrasting with Valhalla's glory, Helheim is a realm of quiet and shadow, where souls lead an existence reflecting their earthly lives. Located beneath Yggdrasil, the world tree, Helheim's gates are guarded by Garm, a monstrous hound.

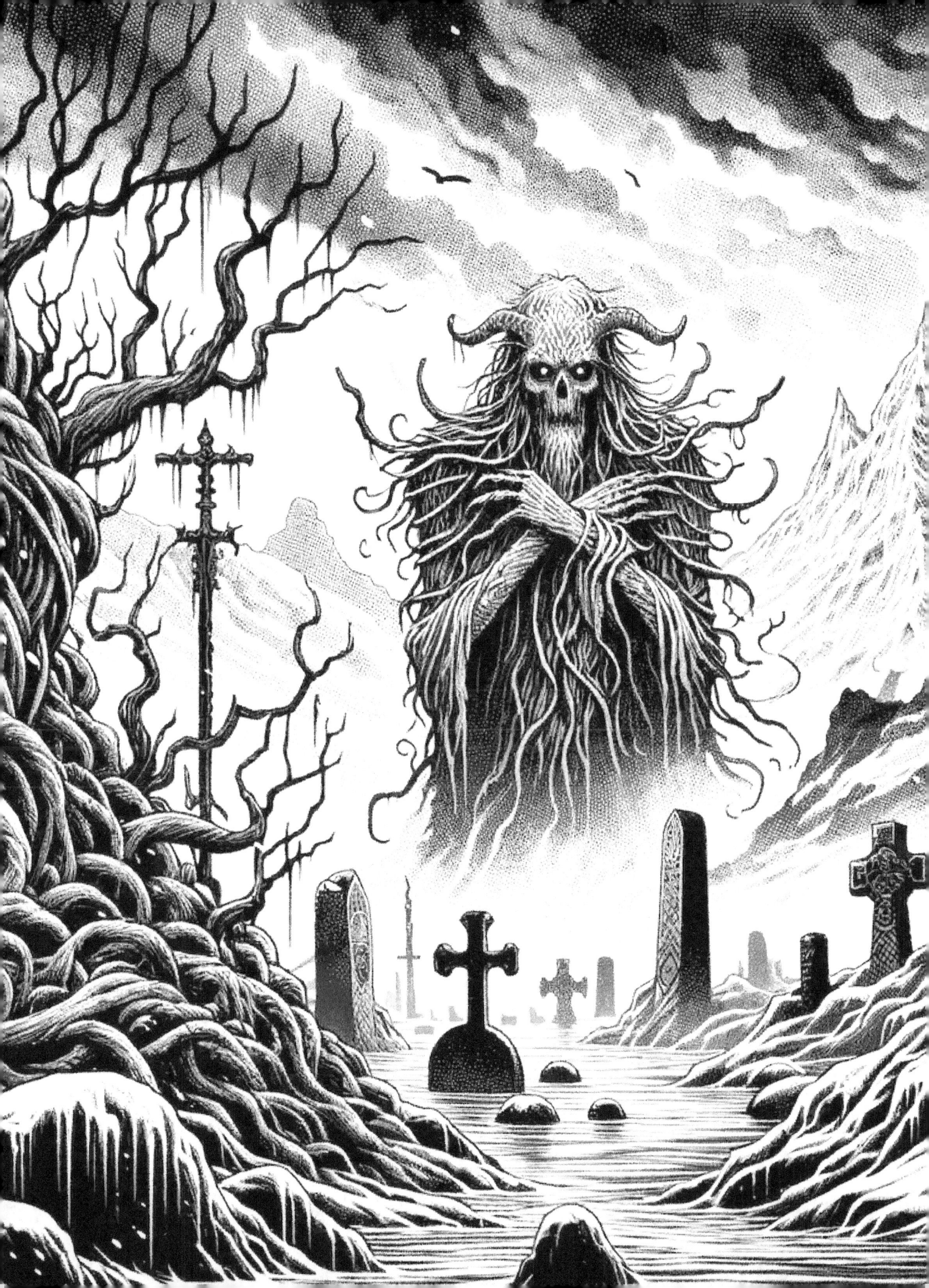

"Garm"

In the shadowy realm of Helheim, Garm, the fearsome hound with gnarled fur and eyes ablaze, stood chained at Gnipahellir's mouth. His growls echoed in the cavernous depths, a relentless reminder of his vigil. These chains, unbreakable and cold, were not just restraints but a testament to his might and the dread he inspired. Each snarl, a prophecy of Ragnarok; each tense muscle, a harbinger of chaos. There, at the threshold of the underworld, Garm waited, a fierce guardian bound by fate, his fury simmering, destined to be unleashed upon the world at the twilight of the gods.

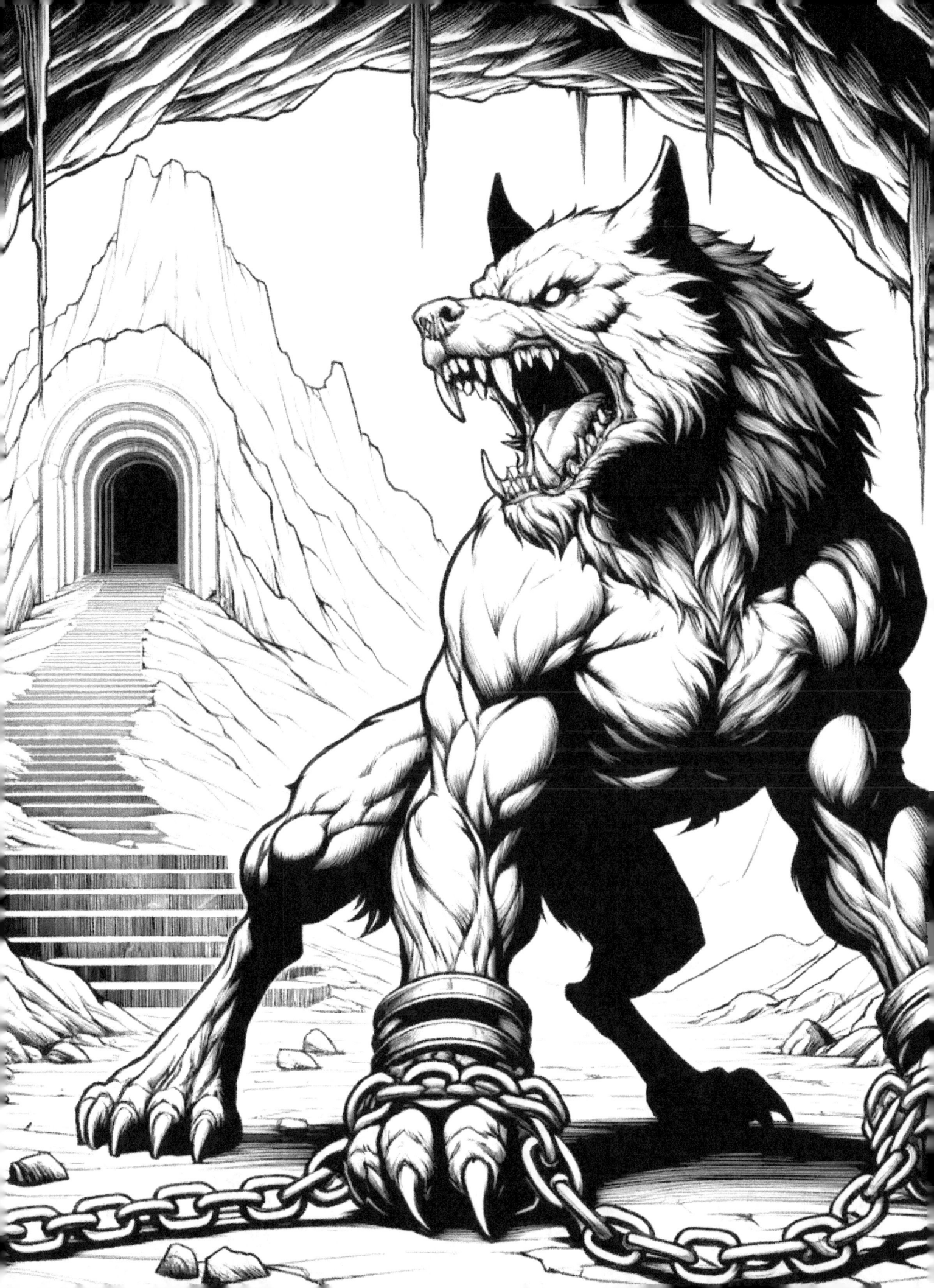

"Rising for Ragnarok"

During Ragnarok, the hordes of lost souls from Helheim, once quiet and subdued, are mobilized for the final cataclysmic battle. Under Hel's command, these forgotten spirits, who spent their afterlife in the cold and dreary underworld, join the forces of chaos. They march alongside giants, monsters, and Loki, embodying the resurgence of chaos against the order of the gods. This spectral army, once deemed unworthy of Valhalla's glory, rises to play a crucial role in the cosmic upheaval, signifying the overturning of the existing order and the blurring of lines between honor and ignominy in the face of ultimate destruction.

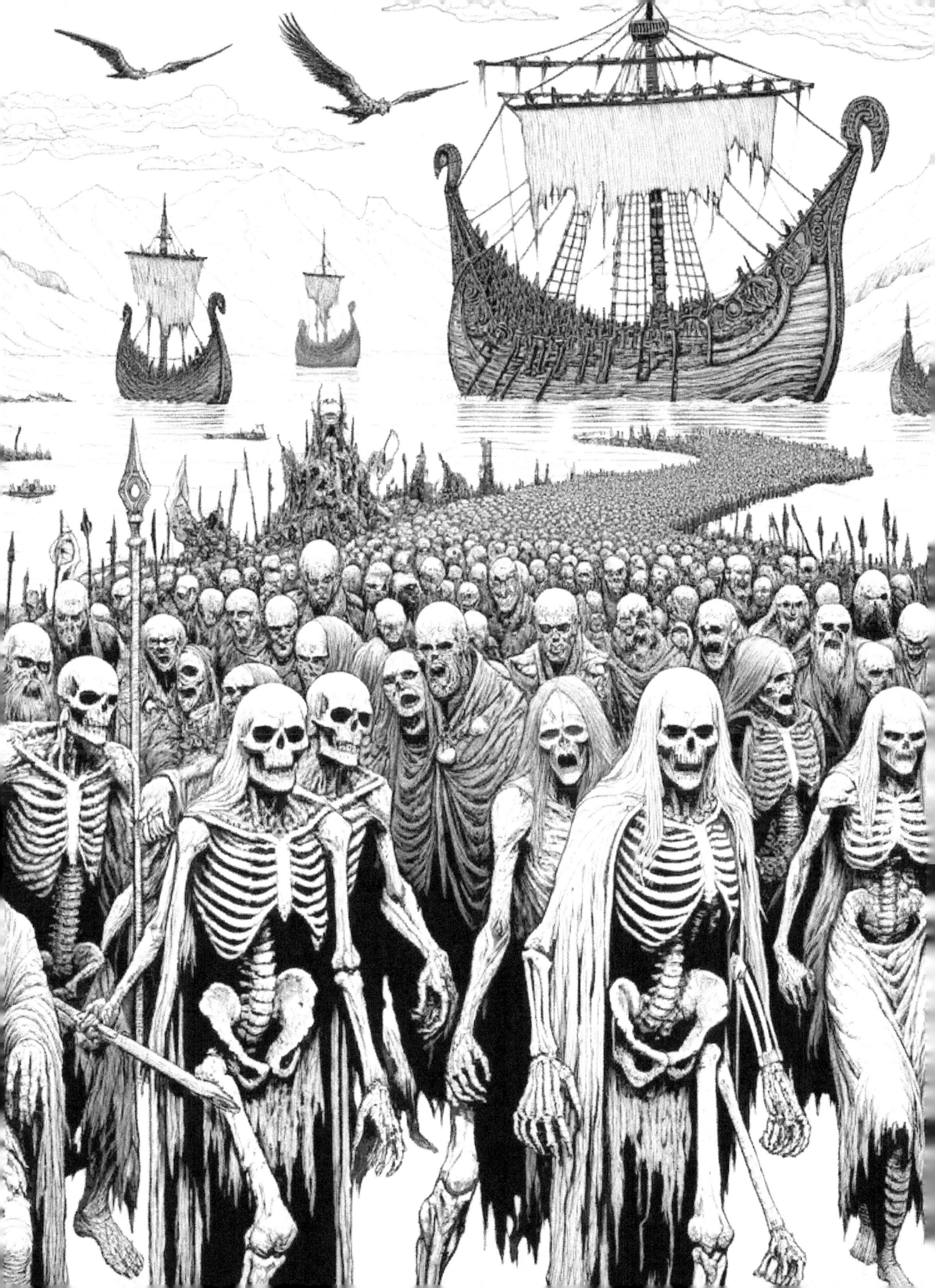

"The Realm of Svartalfheim"

The enigmatic and shadowy realm of the Dark Elves, or Black Elves. Shrouded in near-perpetual twilight, this subterranean world is a labyrinth of deep caves, underground rivers, and hidden forges. The landscape of Svartalfheim is both beautiful and foreboding, reflecting the mysterious nature of its inhabitants.

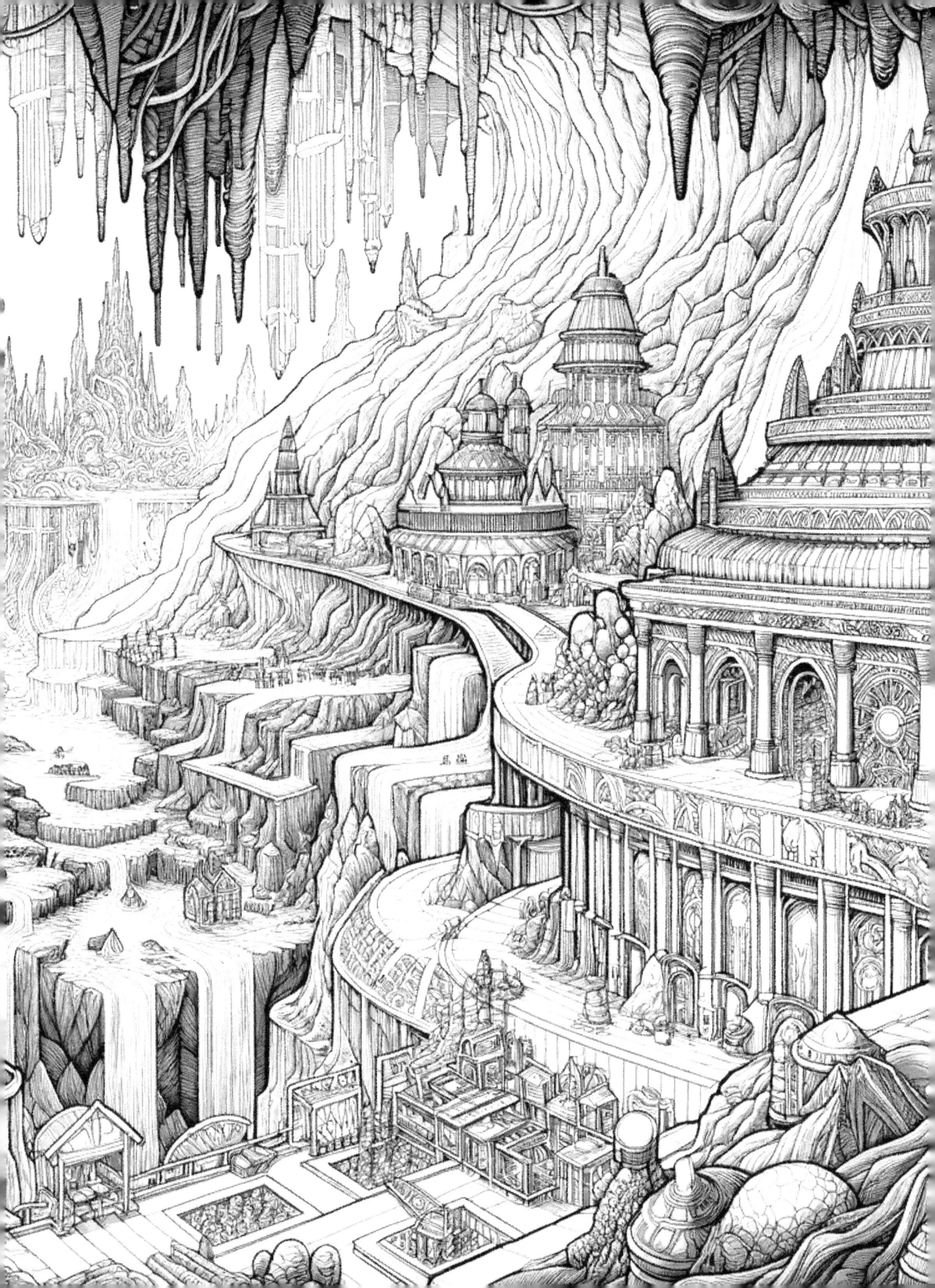

"The Dark Elves of Svartalfheim"

The Dark Elves, or Black Elves of Svartalfheim, are mysterious, shadowy beings dwelling in the subterranean realm of Svartalfheim. Unlike their light elf counterparts in Alfheim, these elves are known for their black magic and craftsmanship. They work in their underground forges, creating powerful and often magical artifacts, like the gods' weapons. Shrouded in the darkness of their world, they are elusive, rarely interacting with the other realms. The Dark Elves embody the darker aspects of elven nature, skilled in the arcane arts, and are masters of secrets, stealth, and subtlety, a stark contrast to the luminous inhabitants of Alfheim.

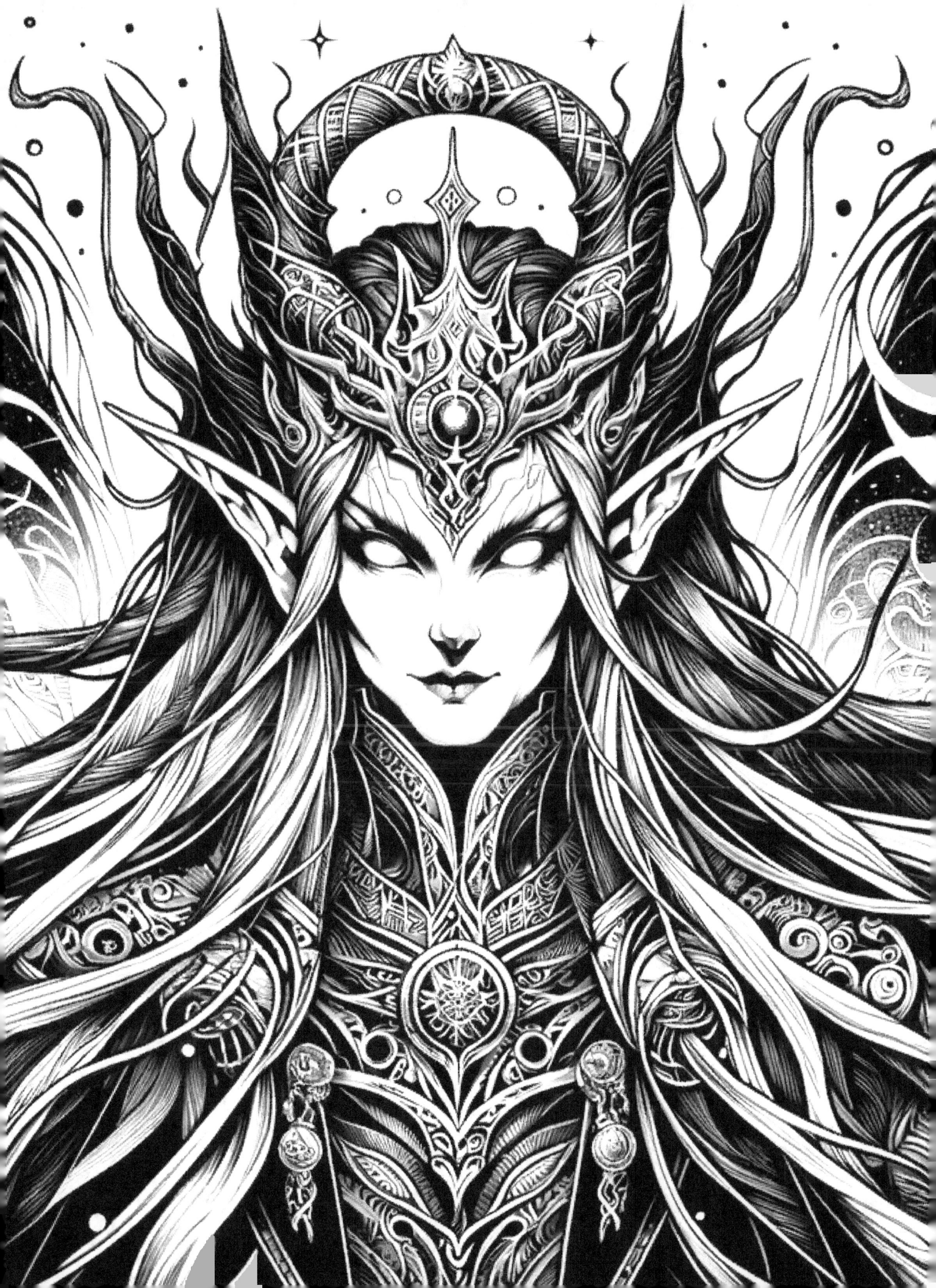

"Nidavellir: The Dwarven Forge"

Often synonymous with Svartalfheim, is the legendary realm of the Dwarves. A world deep beneath the earth, it is famed for its vast subterranean landscapes, illuminated by the glow of forge fires. Here, Dwarven blacksmiths, unmatched in skill, craft wondrous artifacts and weapons, like Thor's hammer, Mjolnir. The realm's intricate caverns and tunnels echo with the sounds of hammers and anvils, as the Dwarves toil, shaping the destinies of gods and men with their creations. Nidavellir is a testament to craftsmanship and the transformative power of artisanship in the ancient Norse world.

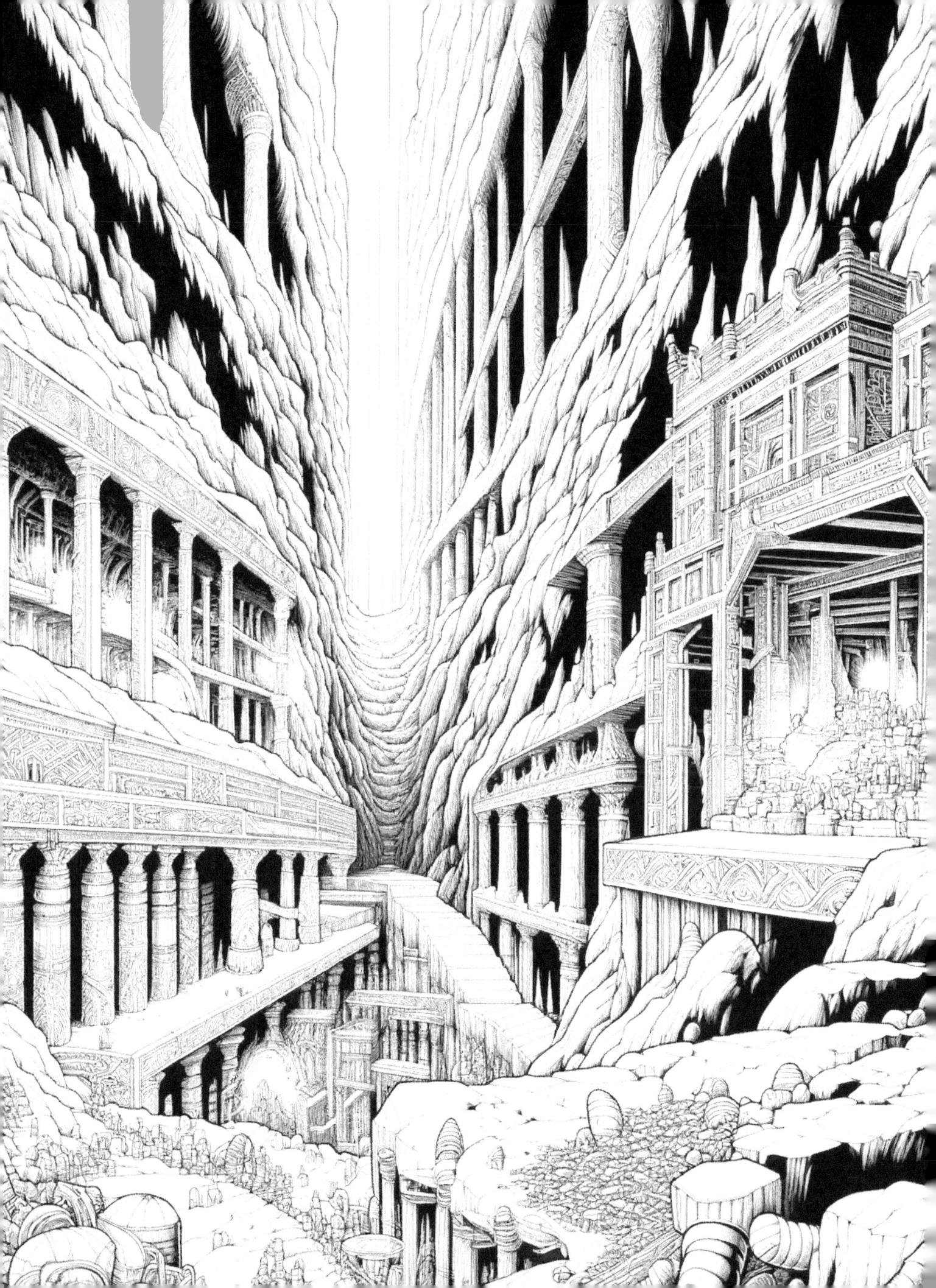

"The Dwarves of Nidavellir"

They are renowned for their unparalleled skills in craftsmanship and metallurgy. Inhabiting the intricate underground realm of Nidavellir, these sturdy, industrious beings are master blacksmiths and artisans, responsible for forging some of the gods' most powerful artifacts, including Thor's hammer, Mjolnir. Dwarves are often described as short, robust, and reclusive, preferring the depths of their forges and the comfort of their subterranean halls. Their keen ability to work with precious metals and magical elements marks them as central figures in many myths, highlighting their profound impact on the balance of power in the cosmos.

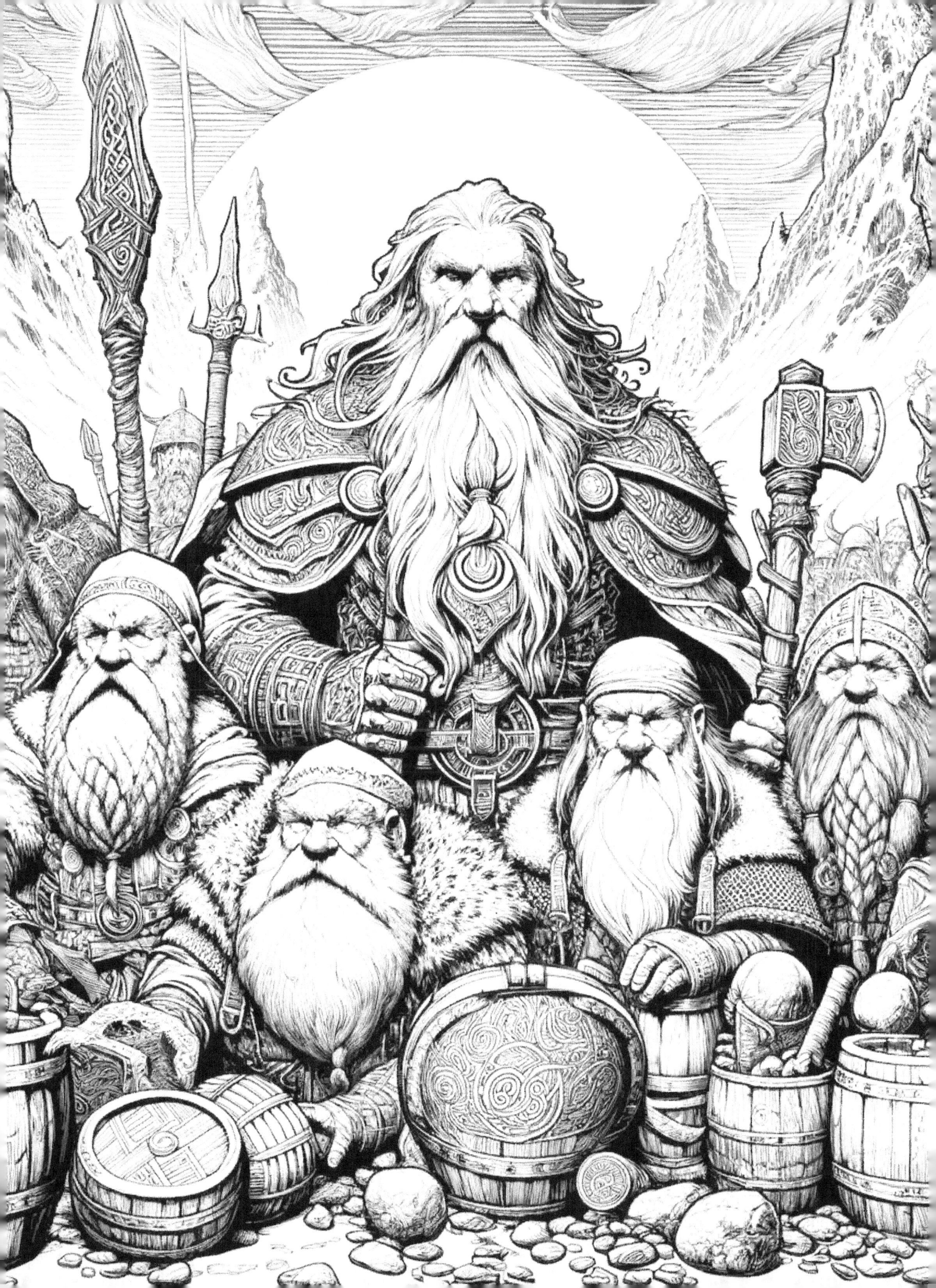

"Muspelheim"

A fiery and chaotic realm inhabited by the fire giants, led by the powerful being Surtr. It is characterized by intense heat, rivers of lava, and constant flames. Muspelheim is one of the nine realms and is situated in the south, opposite to Niflheim, the land of ice and cold. According to myth, it played a significant role in the creation of the world, as the searing heat from Muspelheim combined with the icy rivers of Niflheim to form the primeval void, which eventually led to the birth of the cosmos.

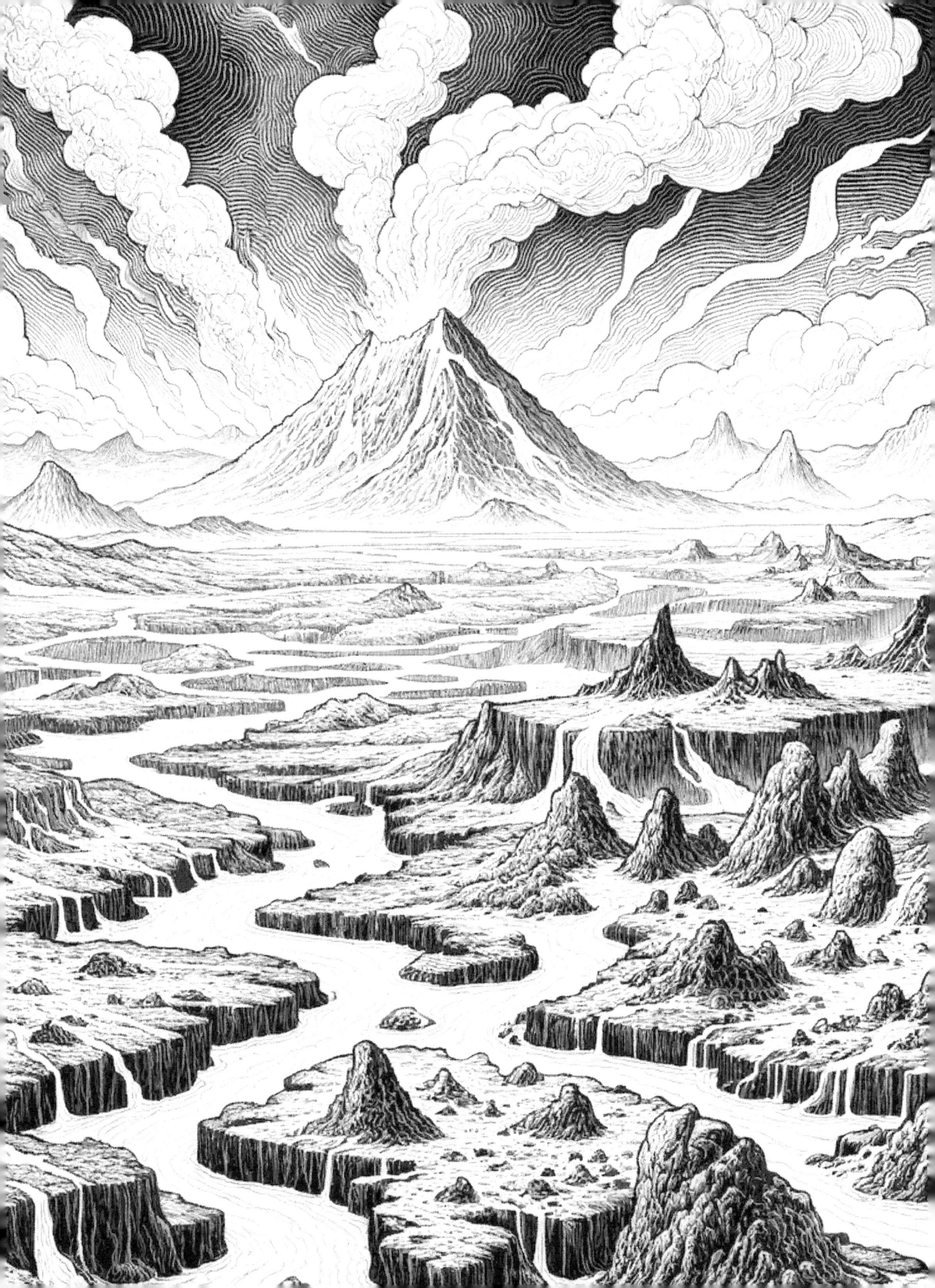

"The Infernal March"

As the apocalyptic event of Ragnarok approached, the fiery realm of Muspelheim stirred with malevolent energy. Surtr, the colossal fire giant king, emerged from the realm's depths, wielding the immense flaming sword, "Laevateinn." His fiery army, composed of fierce fire giants, followed his lead. With each step, the earth trembled and the sky blazed with crimson flames. They marched towards the battlefield, where the ultimate showdown between the forces of chaos and order would unfold. Surtr's arrival signaled the beginning of the end, as flames engulfed the world, setting the stage for the cataclysmic battle that would determine the fate of the cosmos.

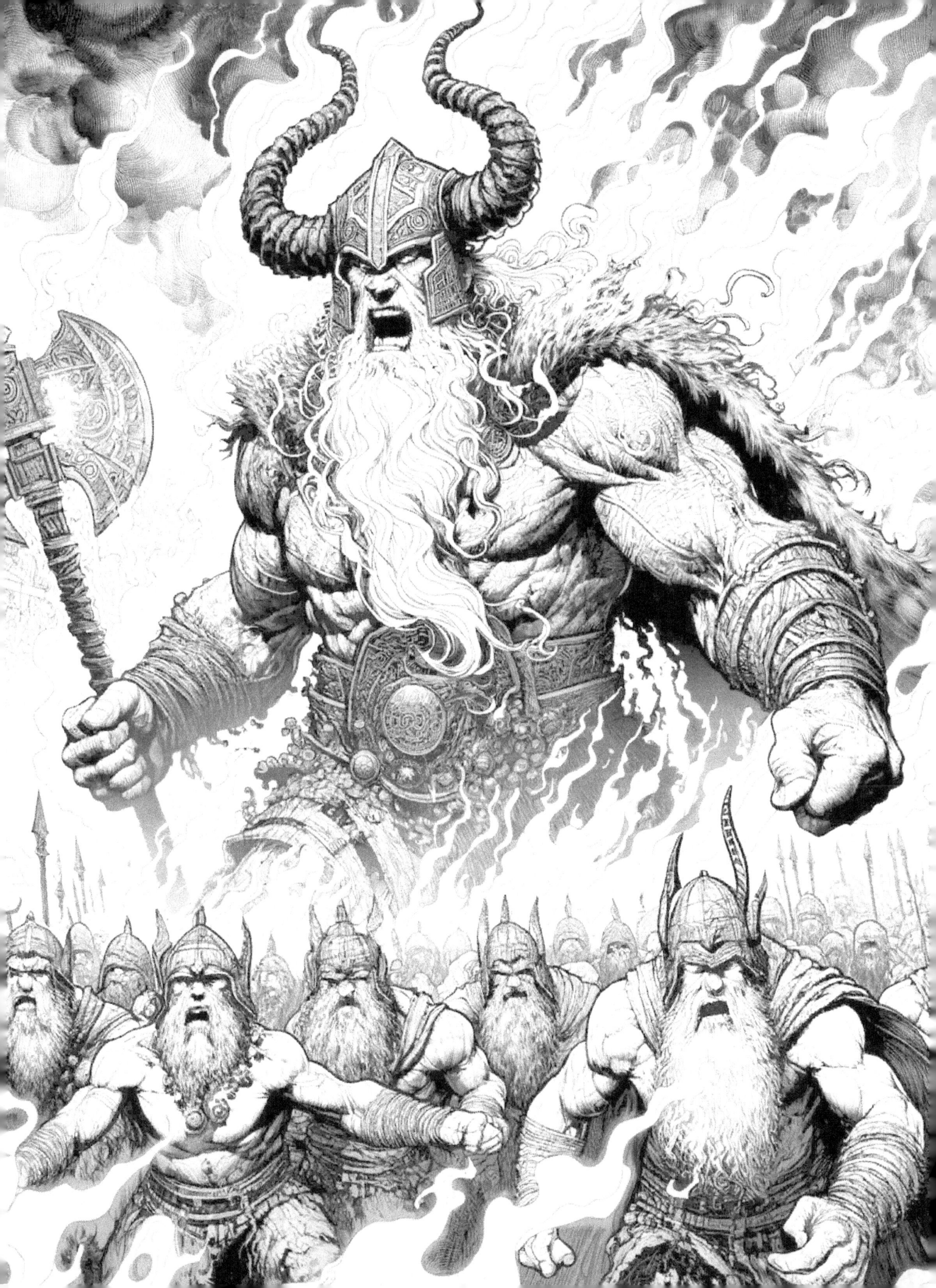

"The Fire Demons of Muspelheim"

Amidst the searing landscapes of Muspelheim, the fire demons, fearsome and relentless, joined the fiery forces of Surtr in the tumultuous march towards the final battle of Ragnarok. These malevolent beings, born of flames and malice, possessed forms that flickered and writhed with fiery intensity. With blazing eyes and scorching breath, they added an infernal zeal to the fire giant's army. As the demons surged forward, their fiery essence consumed all in its path, leaving a trail of devastation. Together with Surtr and his legions, they forged an unstoppable inferno, a harbinger of the world's fiery demise in the cataclysmic climax of Ragnarok.

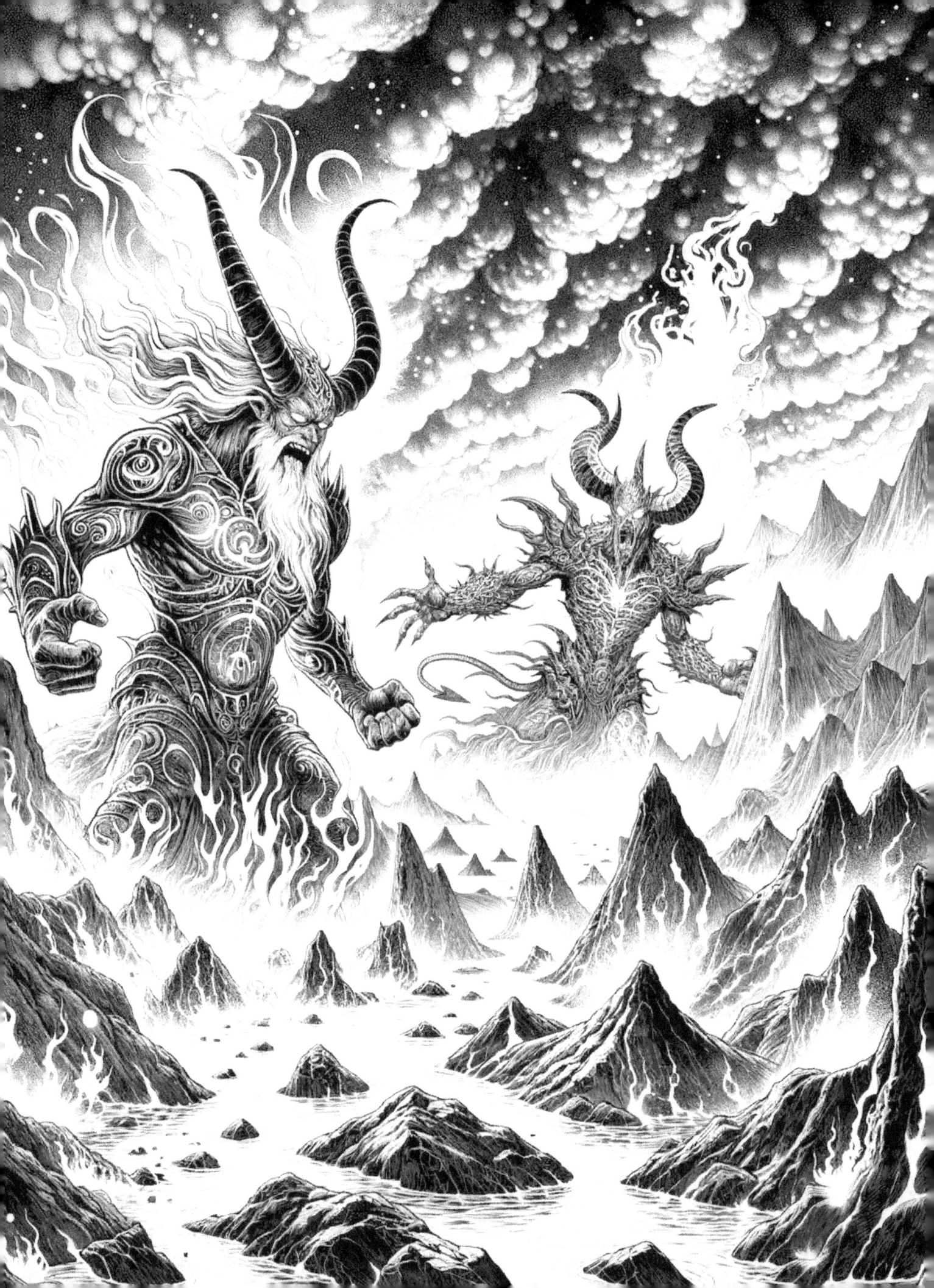

"The Realm of Vanaheim"

The ethereal realm of the Vanir, Norse fertility deities, is a place of lush landscapes and vibrant life. Enveloped in perpetual spring, it boasts vast meadows, blooming gardens, and serene lakes. The air carries the sweet scent of blossoms and the hum of nature's vitality. Here, the Vanir deities, such as Freyr, Freyja and Njord, weave their magic, nurturing the land's bounty and fostering harmonious relationships. Vanaheim embodies the essence of fertility, abundance, and natural beauty, contrasting with the more martial and austere realms of the Aesir gods. It's a realm where the cycle of life and growth thrives in eternal splendor.

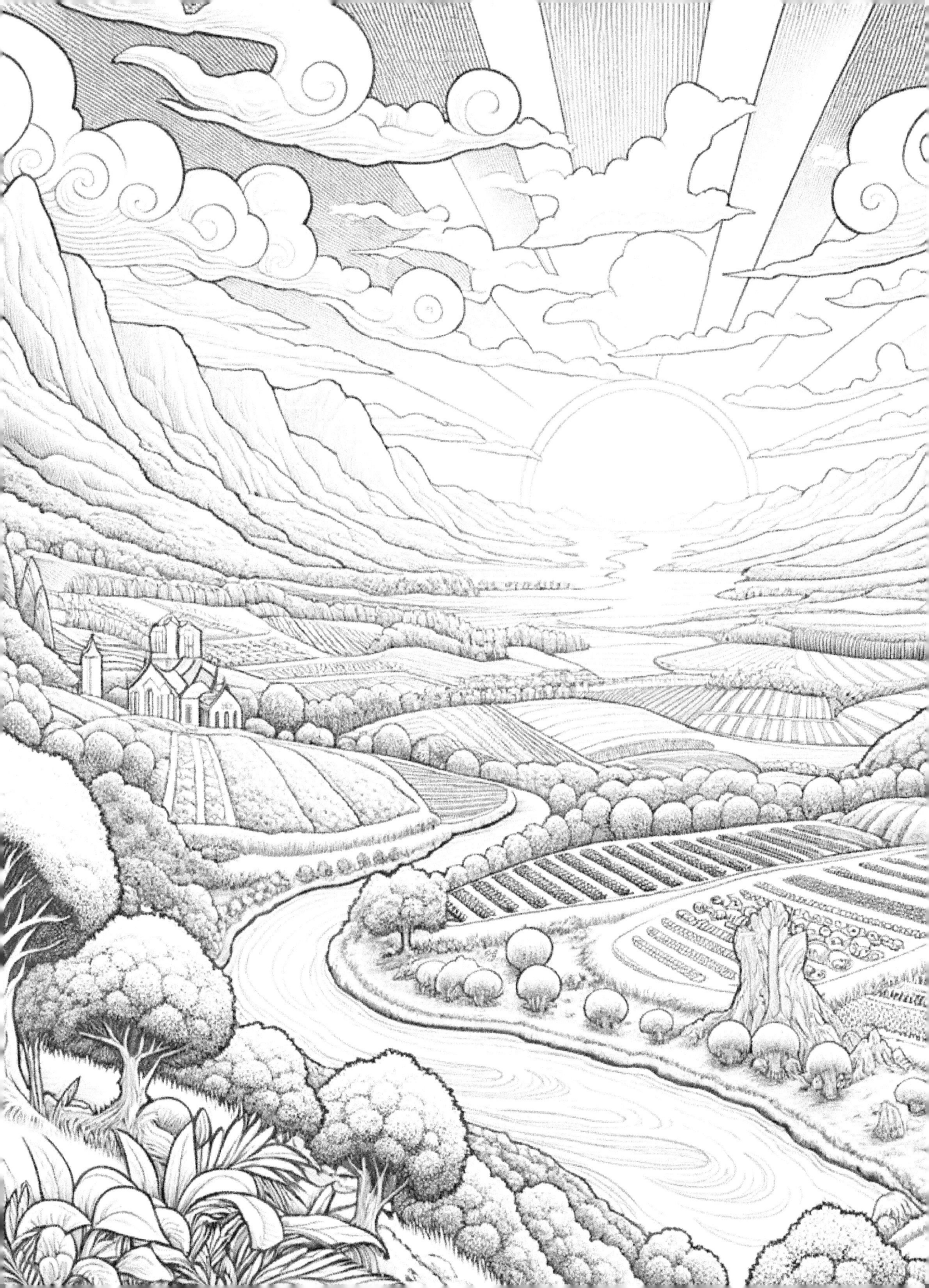

"Freya"

The captivating goddess of love, beauty, and fertility, graced the realms with her radiant presence. Adorned in golden armor and a falcon-feathered cloak, she wears a powerful necklace as a symbol of her allure. Freya's enchanting aura attracted both gods and mortals, and her tears turned into precious gold. A fierce warrior and practitioner of "Seeth" (seiðr), the mystical art of divination, she commanded a chariot drawn by two majestic cats. Yet, her heartache over her lost husband, Od, revealed her vulnerability. Freya embodied the duality of passion and strength, embodying love's enduring power.

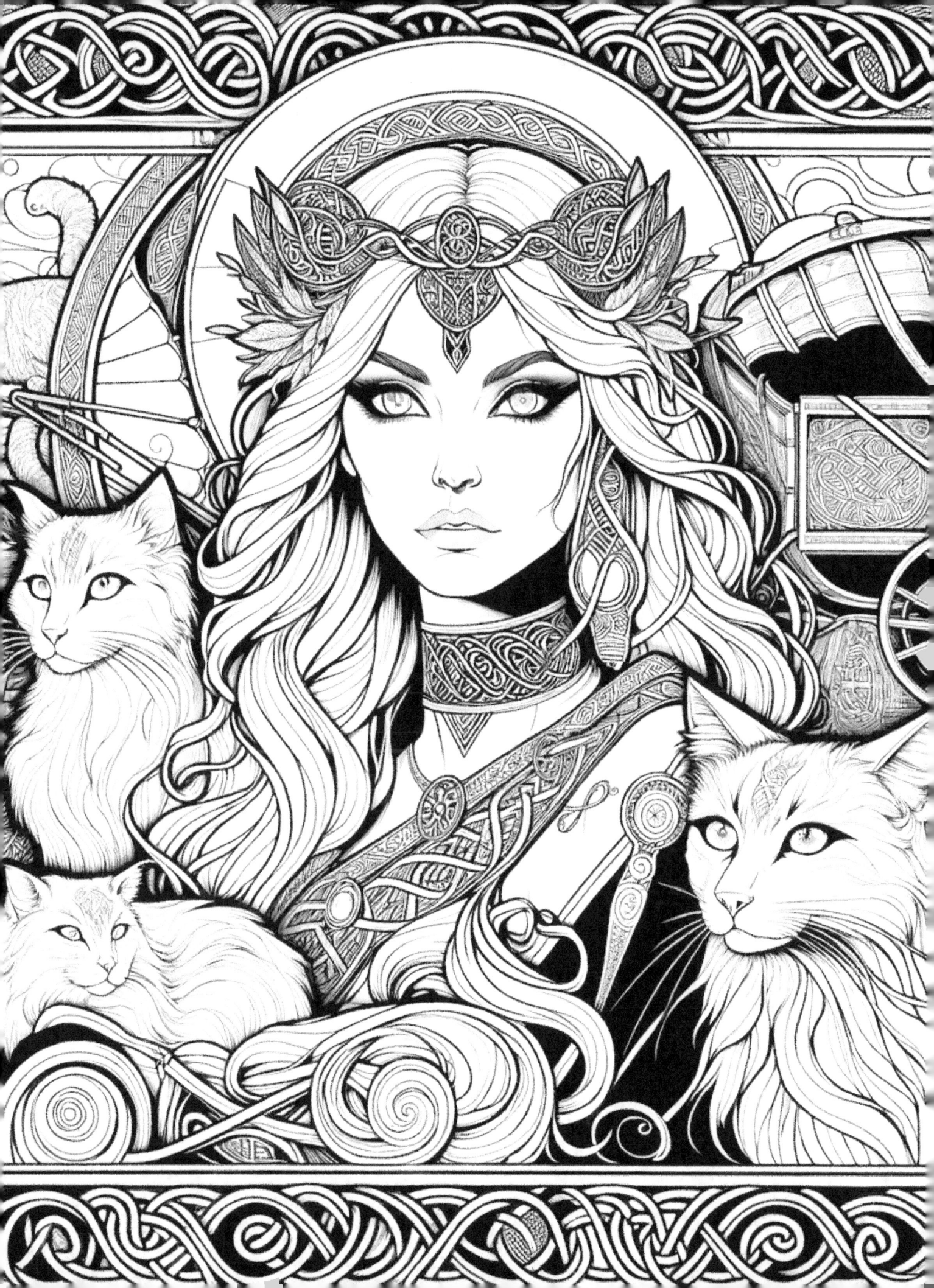

"Njord"

The serene sea god of the Vanir embodied the tranquil beauty of the ocean. His essence was that of gentle tides and salty breezes, and he governed the realms of seafaring, commerce, and wealth. Njord's heart longed for the soothing embrace of the sea, and he often found solace by the shore. As a symbol of harmonious coexistence between the Aesir and Vanir, Njord was married off to Skadi, a giantess. Their union bridged divine worlds, reflecting the delicate balance between land and sea. Njord's presence brought serenity, bounty, and prosperity to those who sought the sea's embrace.

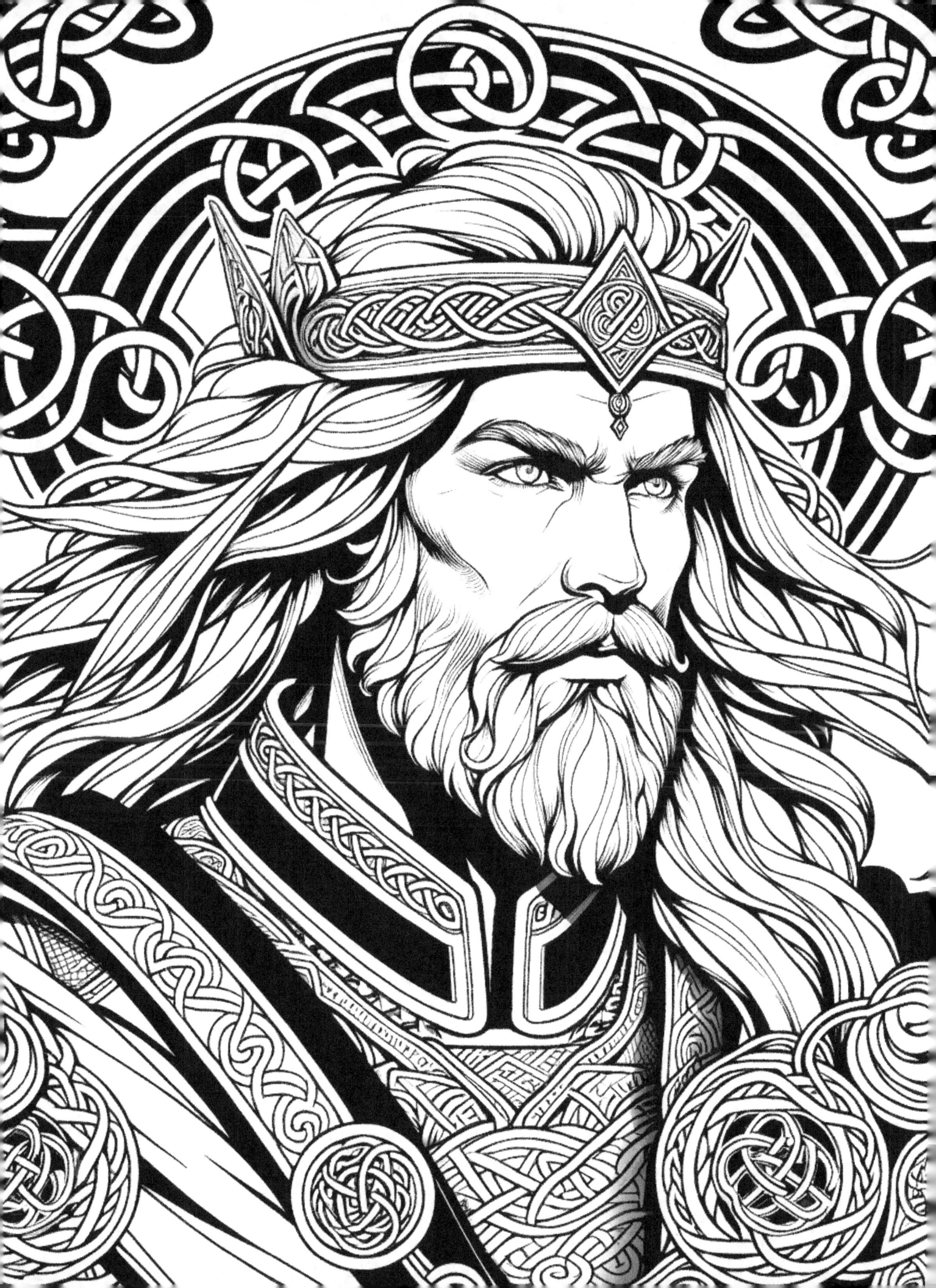

"The Realm of Alfheim"

The realm of light and beauty, where the fair and wise light elves dwell. They are the guardians of nature and growth, and they often help humans in times of need. Alfheim is ruled by Freyr, the god of fertility and peace, who received this realm as a gift from his father. Alfheim is located high in the sky, near Asgard, the home of the gods. It is a place of harmony and joy, where the light elves sing and dance under the stars.

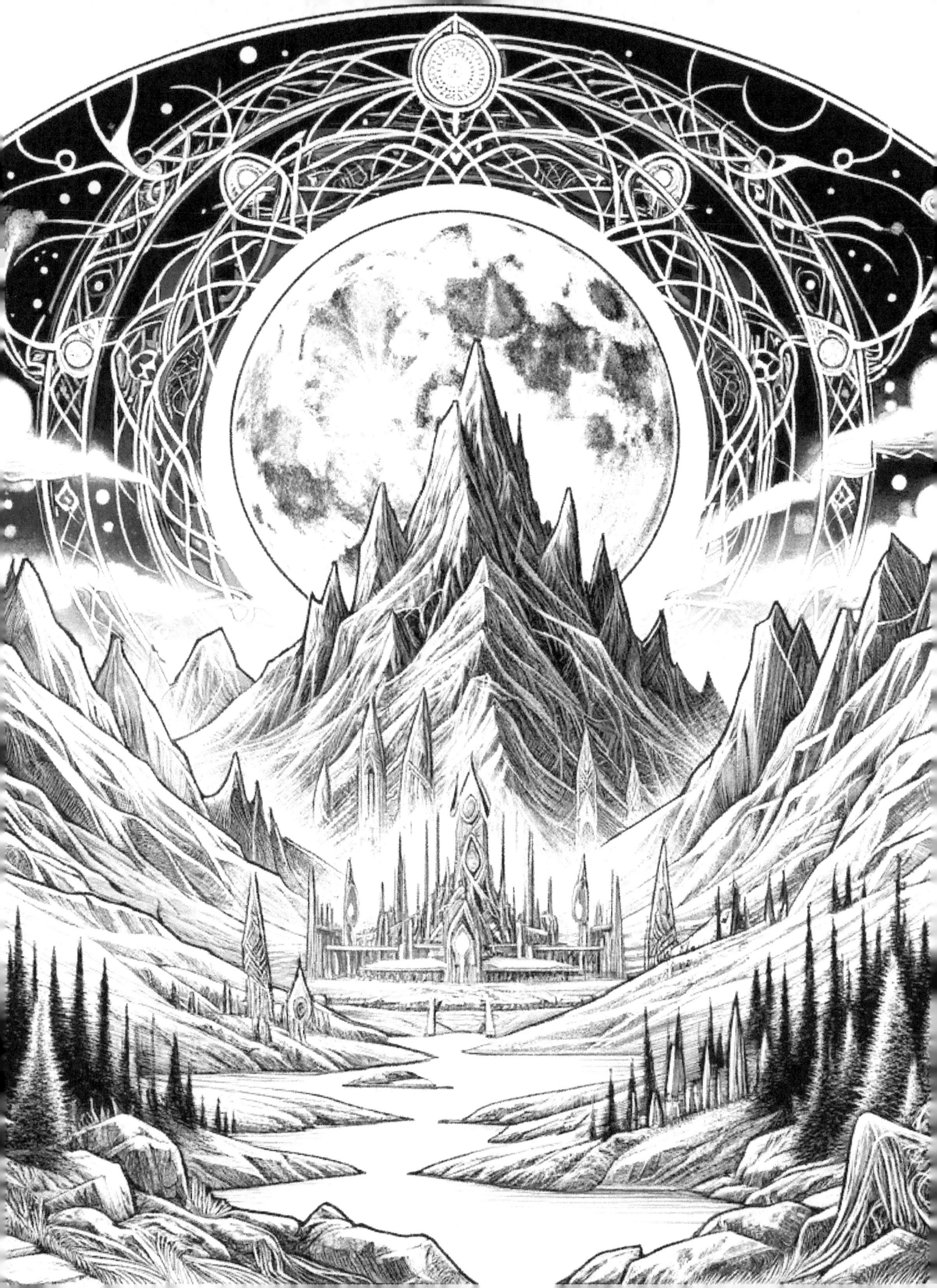

"Freyr"

The benevolent god of fertility and abundance, radiated warmth and compassion. As a Vanir deity, he embodied the bountiful spirit of nature, nurturing crops and ensuring prosperity. Freyr's iconic possession was the magical ship Skidbladnir, which could fold into a pocket-sized vessel and sail on any sea. His most famous artifact, however, was the sword, given by the dwarves, capable of fighting on its own. Freyr's gentle nature stood in contrast to his role as a warrior during Ragnarok, symbolizing both the peaceful harmony of harvest and the valor of protection.

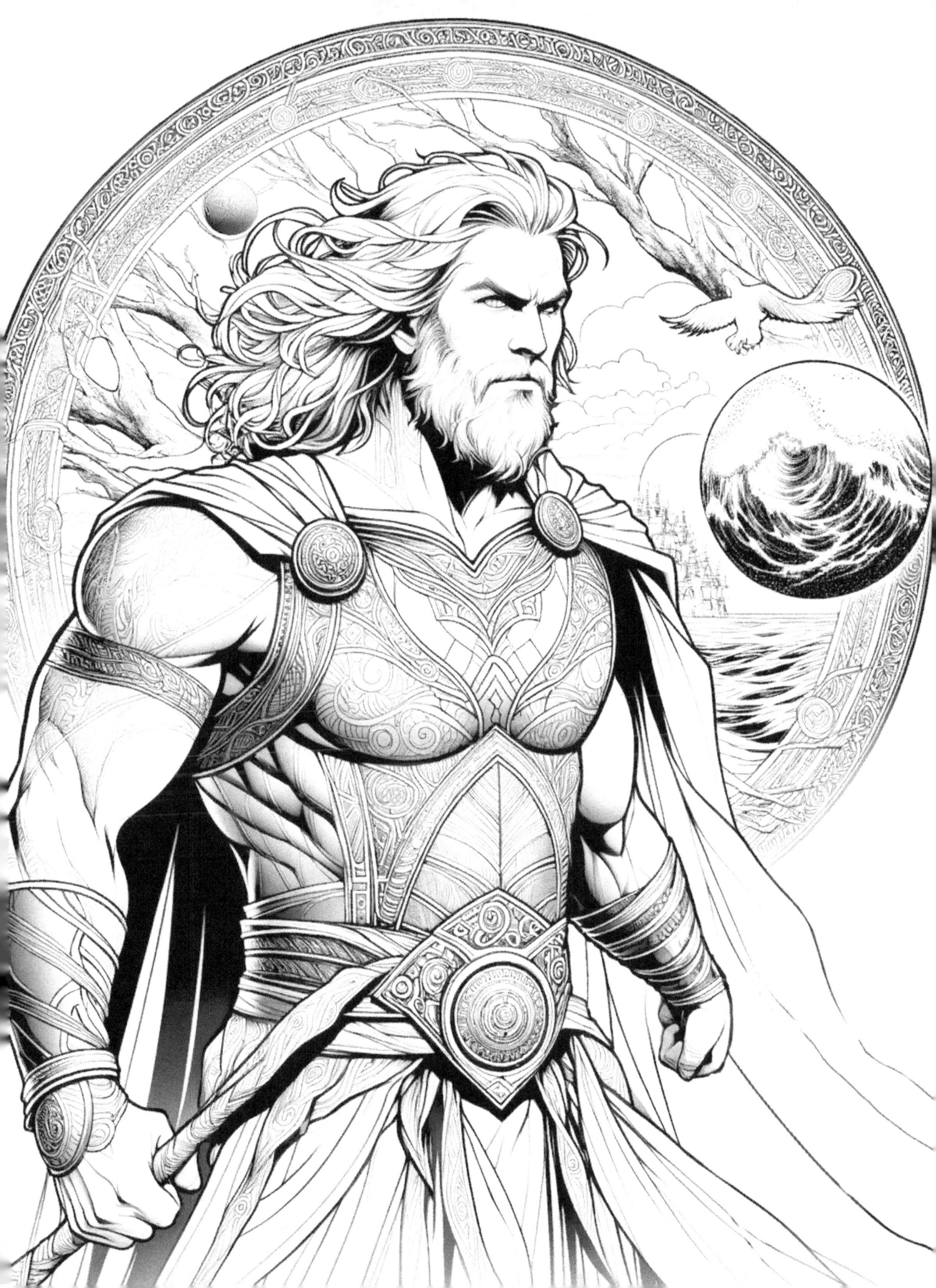

"The Realm of Alfheim"

Ethereal beings who radiate an otherworldly luminescence. Graceful and luminous, they inhabited the realm of Alfheim, where the air shimmered with enchantment. Cloaked in elegance, they possessed an aura of serenity and beauty. Their radiant presence infused the meadows and forests, filling them with life and splendor. Light Elves were the embodiment of purity and grace, their ethereal forms a testament to the enchanting realm they called home. Inhabiting the harmonious side of the cosmos, they stood as guardians of a realm bathed in perpetual light and beauty.

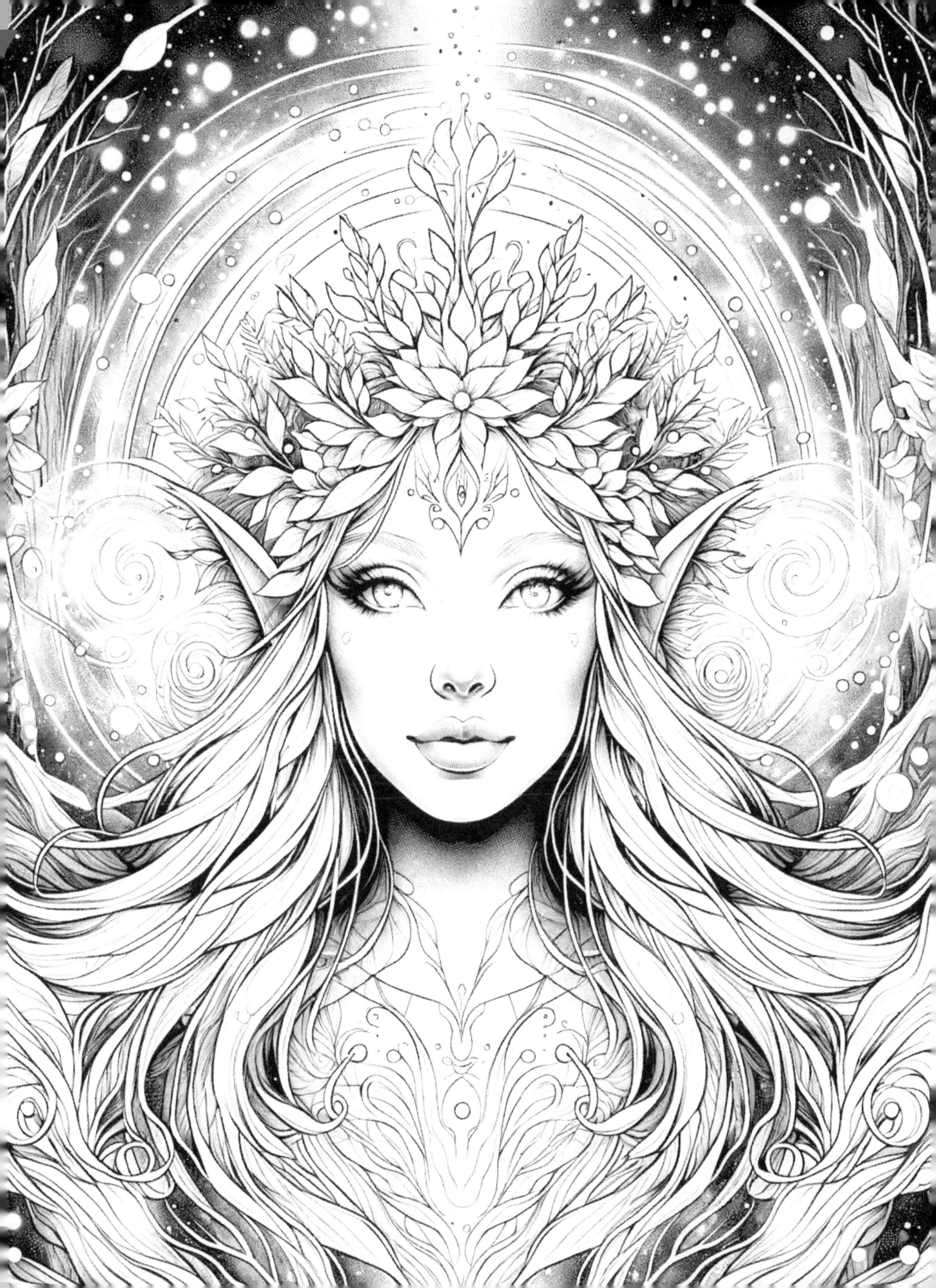

"The Last Battle"

In the twilight of the gods, the Aesir, led by Odin, make their final stand in the apocalyptic battle of Ragnarok. The sky splits open, heralding the arrival of monstrous foes. Odin, flanked by Thor, Freya, and other valiant deities, clashes with the chaos-bringers. Thunder roars and weapons clash; each god fights with fierce valor, knowing their doom is written in ancient prophecy. As the world shudders, the gods and their adversaries fall one by one, entwining their fates in an epic saga of courage, sacrifice, and the inevitable cycle of destruction and rebirth.

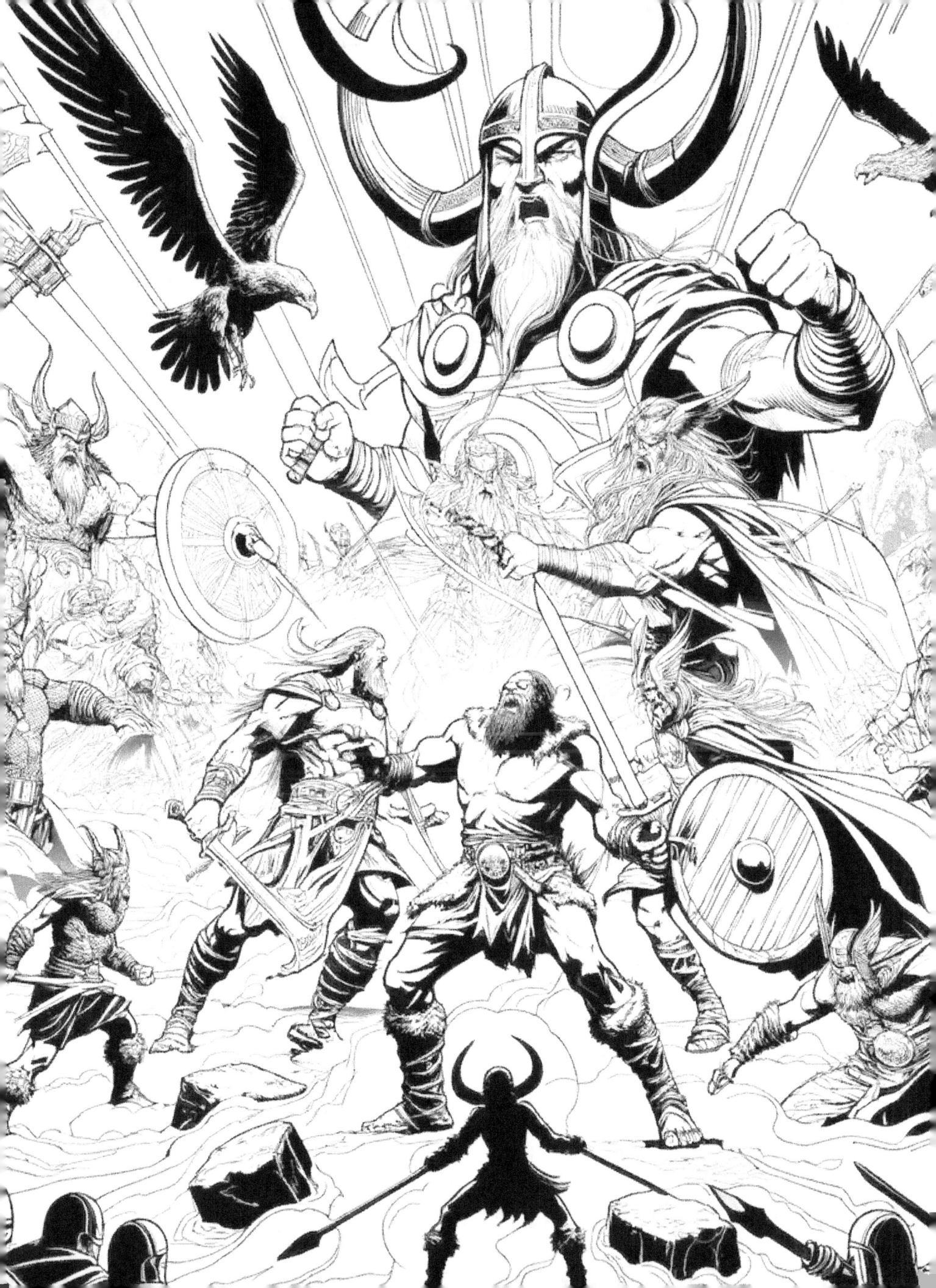

"The Final Whisper of Ragnarok"

In the aftermath of Ragnarok's fiery cataclysm, a profound stillness descends. The world, weary from the chaos, surrenders to a watery embrace. Gradually, the once-mighty trees and towering mountains, etched against a dimming sky, begin their solemn descent. Silently, they slip beneath the gentle waves, leaving whispers of their ancient glory to echo in the depths. As the waters rise, embracing land and sky, the old world relinquishes its form, yielding to a serene yet poignant submersion, signaling an end and a promise of renewal beneath the tranquil seas.

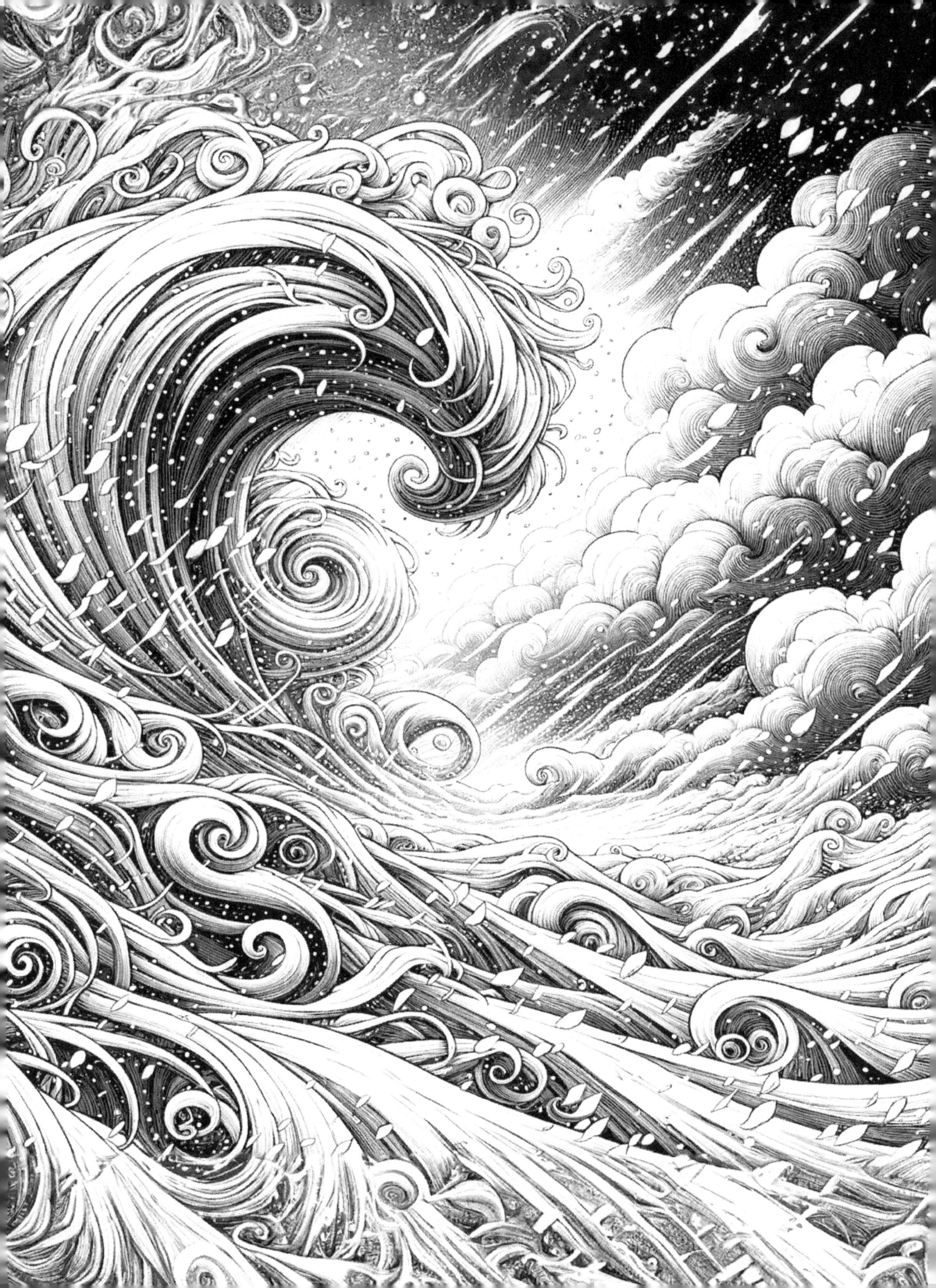

"Rebirth"

After the tumult of Ragnarok, the waters receded, unveiling a world reborn. Fresh, verdant land emerged, bathed in the soft glow of a new sun. Where once there were ruins, now sprouted lush meadows and vibrant forests, teeming with life. In this serene dawn, the air hummed with the promise of beginnings. The cycle of old tales had ended, making way for new stories to be woven. Amidst the gentle rustle of leaves and the cheerful chirp of birds, the world, cleansed and renewed, whispered of hope and endless possibilities in the embrace of a peaceful, rejuvenated existence.

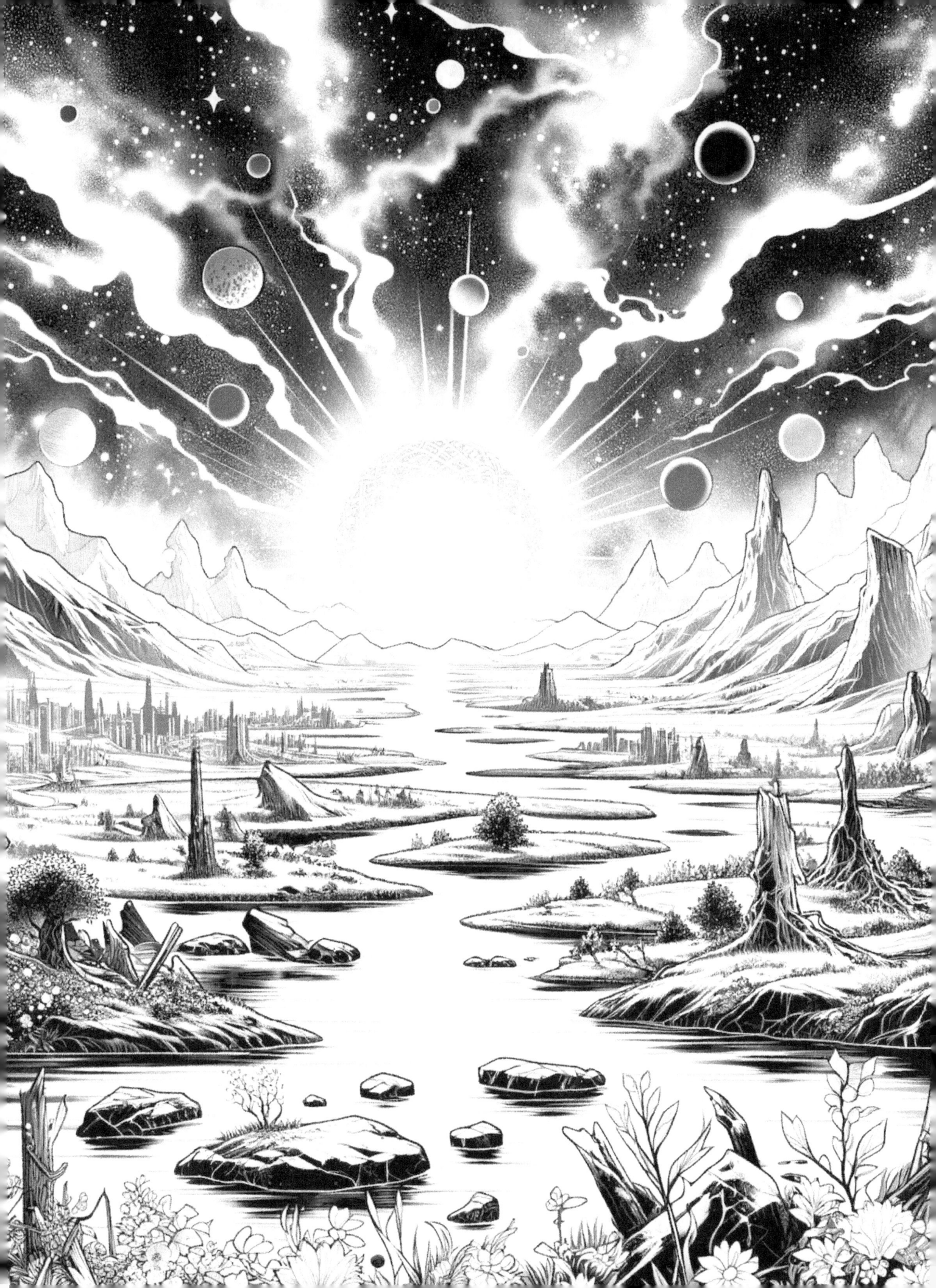